The **Dollhouse Flower Shop**

Flowers and plants from stencilled polymer clay

Publishing Data

First published 2019 Sliding Scale Books (SSPB08)

Plaza De Andalucia 1, Campofrio, 21668, Huelva, Spain.

Illustrations & Photography Angie Scarr & Frank Fisher
Design by Angie Scarr & Frank Fisher

ISBN 9781687037923

Contents

Introduction

When I was very much the same age as my granddaughter will be this December, I woke one morning with my eyes all glued up from sitting in front of the roaring fire the night before, having my long hair dried before my birthday the next day. I could hardly see the wonderful present my mum had made me, but it was my first introduction to dolls houses.

My mum had made me half a dolls house. Just the bottom floor and it was unfinished as were most of the ambitious projects she undertook, as are her daughter's after her. It didn't matter. It was, as everything she did was, a wonderful present. Made with love and care. A simple two rooms and a hallway but it wasn't the inside that interested me, It was the lawn made with green velveteen. The path made with crazy paving patterned Formica and the stonework made with painted sandpaper. and the fact that the modern windows slid up and down but what captivated me then and fascinated me for months after and forms one of my most vivid memories to this day were the plastic roses with detachable heads. I trotted the pipe-cleaner dolls my mum made round the house and made them look out of the window and chat about the roses while taking the red rose heads off and putting them on the yellow roses and vice versa. This was endlessly fascinating to a four year old me.

Of course most of my adult life I have been a miniaturist but I steered clear of flowers. Maybe it was just that I hit upon the caning ideas first and had to follow that as far as it went (into nature of course) before returning to what I realise now was a first love … Originally this book was conceived as a small manual to accompany my stencil kits but as I was playing with other ideas around creating a flower shop it seemed that a proper small book was needed. For this reason you will find a lot of references to our own stencils and products which we developed during a period of my life when I was unable to do my better known caning work.

I first started using a mix of polymer clay and liquid polymer when I was writing my second book where I used it as a 'toffee' coating for mini apples. I've also used it for gluing small parts of my work together in a really permanent way. It works so much better than using any form of glue. The thickness of the mix affects the 'grab', that is to say, the hold of the parts before the glue is set. In this book its used as a stencil medium to create flower petals and leaves which have the thinness of paper combined with a translucency which is not easy with other more traditional flower making methods. There are loads of uses for liquid polymer and my Goo mix in miniature making, some of which I explore in my gardens book, including faux bricks, and textured trees, but this book goes more deeply into an idea I thought up while I was recovering from a recent illness.

Although there are some masterful artists making wonderfully fine work in polymer clay I wasn't one of them so as usual I was searching for an easier way to make something better in a shorter time. Specifically I was trying to make poppies in Fimo to display in the paper 'galvanised' jug kits we were making. My husband Frank had been working on these paper kits with his laser cutter and I suddenly thought maybe he could cut me a stencil that would do the job with my Goo material. After a bit of backwards and forwards in the ideas stage we came up with our first stencil set … then another then another. I was hooked! Now this has become a bit of an obsession for me as its such fun to do and relatively easy to make masses of flowers.

If you don't have our stencils don't worry, you can start by using paper punches to make flower and leaf stencils of your own in light card. Or you can try cutting your own with a craft knife, or if you have a Cricut or Silhouette machine you can make your own designs although some of the more delicate elements can be difficult without a laser machine.

Please note that our stencil designs are copyright although use for your own work is absolutely fine. If in doubt, please ask.

In my "new life" I often make sure anything I do has double or triple value and so I used the making of the flower shop as an opportunity to pass on the excitement of dolls houses and miniature flowers to my own granddaughter, So by way of a dedication the shop in this book along with a copy of the book will be her present when she reaches the grand old age of four.

So, happy birthday Ada. Even though I'm very old now, I remember what it was like to be just four years old! I know there are a lot of other 'nannys' and grandads out there who do too and who are making tangible memories for their own girls and boys.

Making the stencil medium (Goo)

To make a small quantity of Goo you will need a piece of polymer clay in the colour you want your Goo, some liquid polymer, a ceramic tile and a strong palette knife, or even better is a

non-serrated butter knife. Please note that it's easiest to mix basic colours at this stage and then intermix in the semi-liquid state than to try and mix solid colours into the shade you want first. You will need to develop a whole palette of colours for a flower shop but start with a nice deep green and then maybe add a spring green, primaries and white. You will then be able to mix from this palette like any artist!

Chop your clay into the liquid and keep adding more liquid as it becomes dry. This can be quite tiring so don't try to do more than a quarter of a block of

clay at your first attempt or more than one colour mix per day unless you have a handy mixer for the job! I must admit I shortcut the whole process by using a professional mixer but be aware your mixer can't then be used for food and the clay may attack plastic bowls. My mixer has a metal bowl. At a certain point you

will find the mass has a 'scrambled egg' look. You need to keep working, scraping

the knife really flat against the tile so that little by little the lumpiness then the graininess disappears. There is a youtube which shows this at **angiescarr.co.uk/Goo.**

I usually make my Goo the thickness of a non flowing paste, When I want a thinner mix I simply add more liquid polymer. The reason for this is that you can thin a paste out but you can't thicken a thin mix. You need a reasonably flowing mix for most of the stencilling jobs, with the exception of some of the clever colour tricks see page 22. For gluing however its better to have a fairly strong mix which will provide more 'grab.

When you are happy with your mix use the knife to scrape the mix off the tile and into a polymer clay proof container. Small glass jars or small flexible plastic containers will do the job. Don't use hard plastic. Most of the hard/brittle plastics will be dissolved by the solvents in liquid polymers.

Properly stored the mixes should last almost forever although some drying and thickening does occur you can just bring it back with a little more of the liquid polymer.

Tools & materials

The tools needed in this book are, of course stencils. You can find some photocopyable homemade stencils on page 44. and you can also use flower punches to make simple stencils in card.

You will also need

cocktail sticks,
single sided blades,
flower foam (oasis type)
small craft pegs
flower sponge/foam (EVA type)
spatulas
small jars or polymer clay proof tubs
ball tools

To work and bake on you will need tiles (see page 11). An artists smock or work apron will help you stay clean as the Goo we use is very much like oil paint, to clean up you will need kitchen kitchen roll. You can also use wipes but be sure to find biodegradable ones to minimise your non biodegradable waste. We are using plastics of course but there is no reason to compound that by cleaning up with nasty non-biodegradable wipes … You can also use alcohol and baby oil for clean up. You will need baby oil for preparing and cleaning card stencils in any case.

Fabric paints are good for painting flower wire because the heat of baking the flower also sets the paint. You can of course paint the flower wire with green Goo but this can get a bit messy. See more info on flower wires on page 8.

cutting the oasis into a triangle makes it more stable

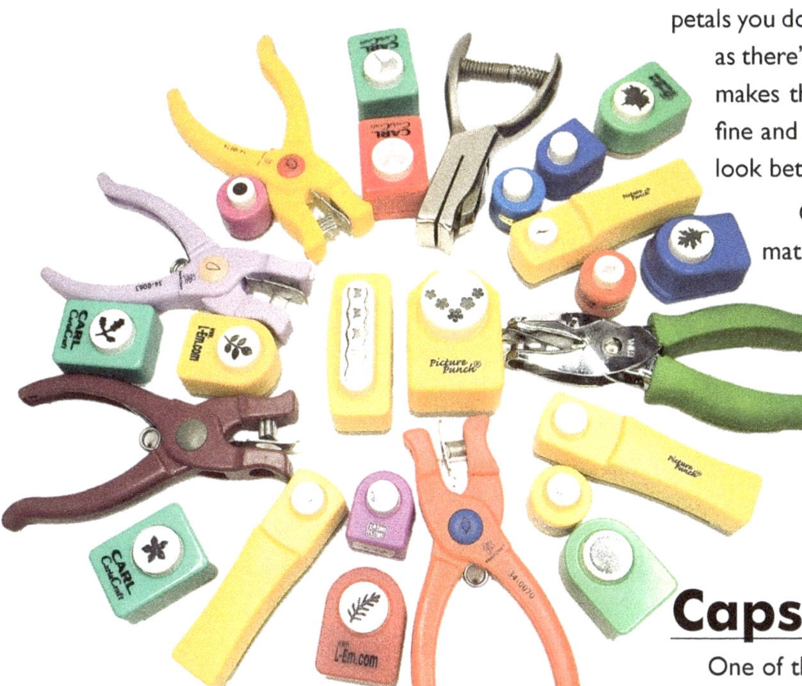

petals you don't need to worry about opacity much especially as there's often a little white in some flower mixes, which makes them more opaque. And the petals can be very fine and delicate and, with just a few exceptions, actually look better when more translucent.

Of course you need to use an oven to set the materials. Use the oven at the median temperature between the instructions on your clay and liquid polymer packs. So, for Fimo with Fimo Liquid it will be around 120 degrees. If your petals break at this temperature raise the temperature by 5 degrees at a time. Everyone's oven is different and sometimes the bake is different on the edges than it is in the middle.

Capsules

One of the tools I use a lot for forming the shape of the petals and some of the leaves is the Vegetarian pill capsule. In reality you could use paper drinking straws but I find capsules are see through so you can see how your flower will turn out. They can also be easily pierced which we do with Tulips for example and cut which I do to shorten them. They are also re-usaable. You MUST use the vegetarian ones because the gelatine ones go crumbly with the heat of the oven. They are sold in sizes 000 (the biggest) to 4 which is the smallest. I haven't seen any smaller but they may be available. You can get them from online pharmacies and drugstores or get small sample packs from our website.

Polymer clay and liquid clay

The medium you use is a mix of polymer clay and liquid clay. There are many types of clay and it doesn't matter which you choose but, especially for leaves you should be careful to find a nice opaque colour because the addition of more than 50% of liquid clay can make it pretty translucent. A little bit of a very opaque white can help with this but will alter the colour tone slightly so its best to start with a good quality fairly opaque clay. As a best all rounder Fimo's leaf green is pretty good but I also like to make my own mixes from the primary colours. More about this later in the book. For flower

Collecting materials

Aside from the Goo you're going to need:

Very small green glass beads for the calyx of some flowers.

Flower wires

The best are the Japanese flower wires but there is quite a nice range from a company called Hamilworth and I'm sure other types are available. Some of the cheaper bulk buys are not very tightly wound so its best to go for good quality. The main range you will need is 24-32 with 24 being the thickest and 32 being very fine indeed. I use 24 for stems of thick stemmed flowers like tulips and gerbera. Slightly finer at 26 for roses for example. For wiring leaves I use a finer wire and for very fine leaves and herbs I'd use the finest I can get which is 30 or 32.

When you're making stencilled or polymer clay flowers, If you don't have the right colour of green paper coated flower wire you can simply paint it, since medium and light green wires are difficult to get hold of. This may be a bit of an obvious idea in some respects. But have you thought of using fabric paints to colour the wires? Fabric paint dries just like ordinary paint so you can handle it straight away but it sets with heat which makes it ideal if you're using polymer clay because it cures with the same heat and this makes it more resistant to moisture. It also seems to make it a little more resistant to unwrapping. When looking for textile paints be careful when selecting greens because some are pretty unrealistic and you may even have to mix your own.

I paint a whole pack at one time by fanning them out on a plastic bag and brushing the paint over them while holding one end. Then I roll them all and brush again. Then obviously I need to let go of the end I was holding and finish that end

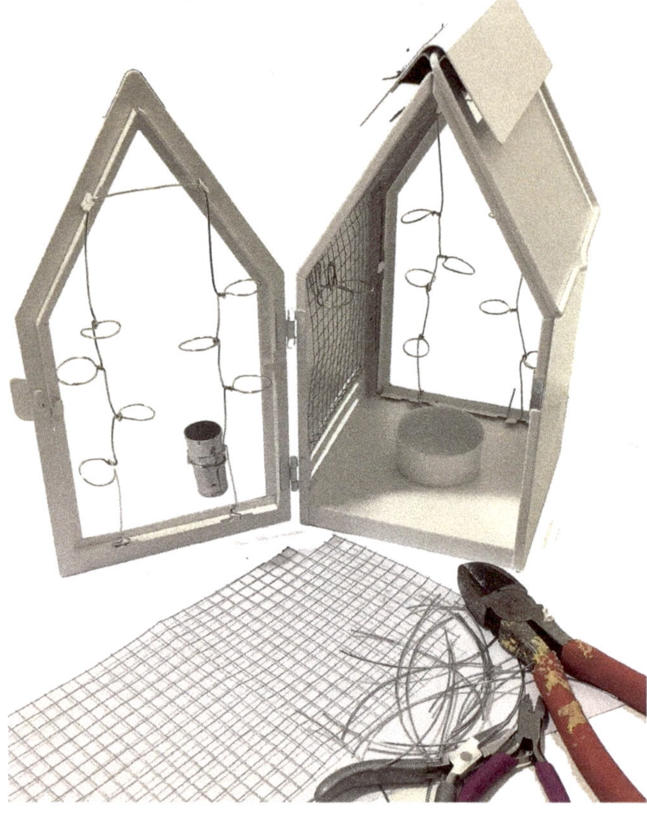

off. When they are dry you might need to touch up a bit but its still a lot quicker than painting stems individually.

Display materials

The making of some buckets and tubs are shown here on page 44 but you can also start collecting mini flower pots and tubs and vases etc . There is a Spanish company called Mibako who make lovely little plantpots wholesale. You can contact them for a list of suppliers. Some beautiful handmade pottery vases can be obtained from Elizabeth Causeret a French specialist in miniature pottery.

Finding your 'shop'

Obviously you can just make a pot or bunch of flowers as a stand alone item. A collectable gift for a friend or something for your mini garden. But what if you're really loving it and want to make a whole shop full or just a little display of your work, well here are a few ideas for you.

You can buy ready made market stalls or make your own using the pattern in my first book Making Miniature Food and Market Stalls.

a real flower stall in Malaga

Or you can buy a shop kit (details in the supplier pages) I was lucky enough to persuade my Aussie friend Andrea to let me have one of the flower shop kits she uses for classes as a lavender shop. I made my version a bit more modern and cleaner because I wanted to display more flowers in a more contemporary setting. Another really lovely idea is to use ready made lanterns, or mini cactus greenhouses. In this little white lantern from Ikea I've made some wire walls to hang flower tubs from rings and further wire pot holders for the front and back windows so it looks more like a little flower stall. I also raised the floor around the candle holder and used the holder for a topiary tree in my final display.

While looking at lanterns as a display I found these little brass ones in European chain:

Action. They are very tiny and very inexpensive but perfect for a little collection of plants. And the slightly bigger octagonal one I also thought was very pretty for a collection. A bigger lantern such as this one below would be big enough for a full size street vendor flower stall! The roof certainly reminded me of the real flower stall, in the picture below left, which I saw in Malaga. See project 12 on page 42 for a medium sized one.

Making a lot of flowers

To make a lot of brightly coloured flowers as quickly as possible I recommend that you use my stencils although you can make your own from flower and leaf shaped craft punches. And some people prefer making flowers with paint and paper. Whatever your chosen medium I hope you get some inspiration here.

Basic stencilling. why and how

Why stencil? Because you can get a very clear edged shape without resorting to scissors and you can work very small without resorting to paper and punches and the strain of using those materials. Because you can colour without applying thick paint over and you can maintain translucency or add opacity. Stencilled flower parts are also flexible and pretty durable when baked properly and can be re shaped using heat afterwards. You can stencil now and store plant parts to use later and because its such fun to produce an infinite umber of shades of colours so easily. The colour stays in the holes but scrapes off the stencil. When you lift the stencil carefully, hopefully you will leave behind a perfect imprint.

How to make your own stencils.

You can use paper punches to create a whole range of pretty flowers and leaves on card. The drawback is that because the punches are short on 'throat depth' its difficult to get the flowers or leaves the right way up so that the small elements don't catch when you're stencilling. But if you're just making a few and you own the cutter anyway so can replace damaged card stencils easily, it really doesn't matter. You can create your own designs again using thin card and cut them out using a sharp scalpel. This is more time consuming but the positive is you can work towards your own exact design.

If you are lucky enough to have your own plotter machine you can also create your own designs on card.

There is a design for rose leaves and a few other designs that you can copy onto card on page 44. You can cut them out with a scalpel.

Care and cleaning of card stencils.

Absolutely the best way to care for a card stencil if you want to use it again is to prepare the stencil by coating it with Baby oil. Allowing it to soak in and removing the excess oil by blotting with a piece of Kitchen roll. Be sure not to catch any delicate parts.

Although card stencils should be considered a one + use tool meaning that you can use it more than once if you really take care of it you do have to follow certain rules for using as described on the following pages. After use if your stencil is not damaged you can clean it by removing excess clay from round the edge of the card and then using baby oil to carefully remove the remaining Goo from the main part of the stencil. Store flat or slotted back to back in a box for further use.

Bought stencils

The advantage of buying your stencils is speed of production and confidence in the quality. You know we've done the research and development on the designs and tested them, and they work. The card ones are still '1+ use'. And I advise making a good quantity of your chosen flower or leaf the first time out in case you damage them in cleaning or storage.

The flexible plastic Professional ones don't need any preparation and can also be easily cleaned using baby oil. You still have to be careful not to damage smaller parts by being very careful to follow the "how to use your spatula" information on page 13 (troubleshooting) and cleaning in the same direction as any small spikes and sticking out bits. Every effort has been made to minimise these but some plants are so complex and delicate some mistakes will be made but never fear. You can replace single stencils by quoting the unique reference on the bottom.

Sometimes these can be difficult to read depending on the cutting techniques we have used so we can help you if you have any problems.

Clean up after stencilling

In addition to cleaning the actual stencils your tiles may be smeared with extra Goo. Scrape up any useable Goo and return to the pot. Mixed colours can be put into different pots. Clean the surface with disposable kitchen wipes or hygienic wipes. Or paper towels and cleaning alcohol or baby oil.

If you accidentally splash your clothes with Goo or liquid polymer use alcohol to blot clean.

Tiles for stencilling on

From now on I will use the words printing and stencilling interchangeably.

There are several kinds of tiles you can use to print on. From experience I list the worst to the best here:-

Small shiny wall tiles

Too small to do much work on and one side of your print will be too shiny and unrealistic.

Matte wall tiles

The matte tiles are better because the shine is reduced but can still be a bit shinier than I like.

Slightly 'gritty' floor tiles

Avoid too much grit because they add too much texture and the flower parts are more difficult to remove. On the other hand they are less shiny and some texture may be interesting on certain types of leaves.

Unglazed terracotta

Unglazed tiles are my current favourite. They leach excess oils from the Goo minimising shine to almost nothing. One drawback is that over time your tile will be too oily and this effect will reduce. They are usually pretty cheap but can be difficult to find since they are more common in Mediterranean homes than in northern Europe. The bigger ones are very thick and heavy.

You need to bake these tiles soon after using and not leave them until the next day as they absorb the material a little.

Stencilling basics

If your stencil is made of card, be sure to wipe it with baby oil before using. This makes it easier to clean and longer lasting.

Apply baby oil to the whole of the card then dab off any excess. Don't stencil with a visibly oily card.

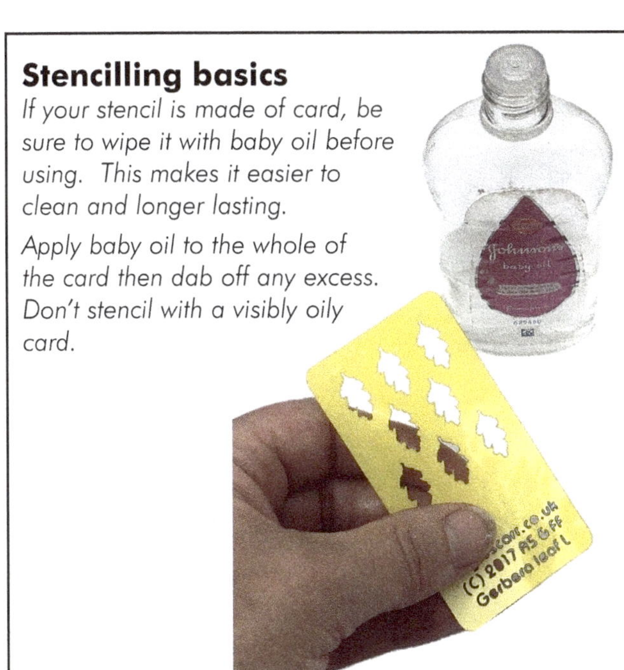

Project 1a: start stencilling and wiring leaves

You will need:

Some stencils either from my range or you can make your own using punch cutters.

Leaf green Goo (see page 5)

Paper coated flower wire. Use thin wire approximately 28-30 gauge for the leaves. If you're only buying one pack for both flowers and leaves, go for 26 gauge.

You will also need a matte ceramic tile and a spatula to apply the Goo.

Cut flower wires to 2.5 - 3cm lengths and dip into some Goo so it smears along the length of the top half of the wire. (6) Apply the wire to the back of the leaves (7) and bake again. If you find your leaves are too translucent try another brand of clay or apply the Goo more thickly.

Bake the leaves again. (8)

Gerbera leaves

Take a spatula full of your Goo and apply it to the top right hand corner of your tile or on to another tile. Mix it down with a little more liquid polymer if it isn't already soft like thick cream.

(1) Hold the stencil firmly to the top right hand side of your tile by the bottom edge (you may beed to swap the sides if you are left handed).

Ensure it does not slip. Scrape a little Goo onto the underside of the spatula and put it across the stencil just below the flowers and above the name print (if its one of mine). (2) Holding the stencil down really firmly by the print end, draw your spatula upwards from the bottom of the stencil to the top at a gentle angle (3) (4) so as not to catch the card that separates the leaves. Lift the stencil carefully and replace it underneath the first print to continue printing. Work your way down the tile to the bottom and then start a new line of prints to the right of the first. Bake the leaves on the tile at the median temperature between your liquid clay and your clay's recommended temperatures for the recommended time.

Remove the leaves from the surface with a single sided blade (5) and if the backs are shiny turn them shiny side up.

Stencilling Troubleshooting

Don't load your spatula and stencil with too much Goo at once. Get used to cleaning the spatula off on your tile between strokes/scrapes. Make sure your Goo is really well mixed. A granular mix will not stencil well.

Make sure your tile is really clean and has no residue from your last stencilling job. Even the tiniest bits of old clay can 'drag' though your current job leaving an empty line and thus 'split' a petal or a leaf.

Tiles should ideally almost fill your oven with just enough space around for air to circulate. This is to maximise the area of tile you can bake on at once. Be aware that your oven may have cold spots. Where cold spots happen your Goo may not bake well and may be crumbly.

Different clays and liquid clays bake at different temperatures. I usually take the median temperature between any mixed materials therefore I'll generally bake Fimo and Fimo liquid at 120 degrees C (250F) or a little more. If you find your work is under baked you can set the oven higher and bake again.

If you under bake elements they will crumble.

If the Goo is too thick it may pull and bend small parts on the stencil and be difficult to remove from the stencil.

Stencils have starting and stopping points but any Goo that gets accidentally scraped over the edge can be cleaned off with the spatula.

Make sure the angle of your spatula is around 45 degrees. Some stencils may work better with a lower angle but a higher one will catch small parts.

Once you have damaged a stencil its difficult to use again. You can clean it and turn it over (if appropriate) so that raised bits are now pressed down. However a badly damaged stencil will need replacing. You can replace single Angie Scarr Miniatures stencils individually. Just request the stencil using the details from the original.

Project 1b: Gerbera flower

If you haven't done the leaves first please look back for stencilling method.

Top tip
Make sure you have 2 thicknesses of your chosen colour your first mix should be thick (for gluing jobs) and then you should mix down a slightly thinner mix by adding a little more Liquid Fimo for stencilling.

(1) Just as with the leaves, the colour stays in the holes, but scrapes off the stencil. Lift the stencil carefully, hopefully leaving behind a perfect imprint. If it is imperfect simply scrape

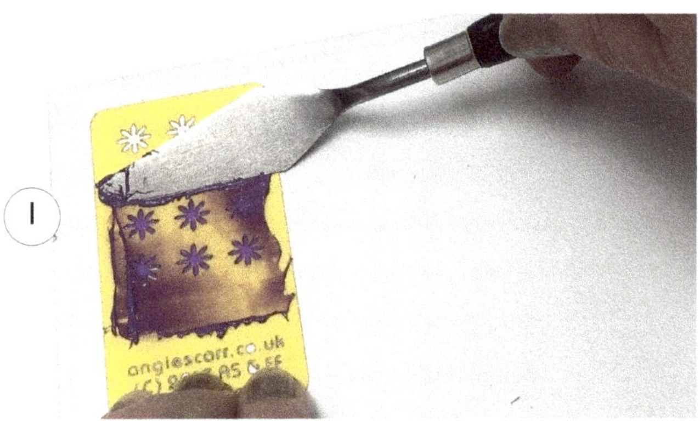

the Goo off, wipe down and apply again.

After filling the tile, stick a small holed bead to the back of around a third of your petal parts using a cocktail stick or pointed tool to pick each bead up and then a smear of thick Goo on the bead. (2) If you have good fingernails this should be easier! Simply push the bead off the cocktail stick into the flower with the same hand that you're holding the cocktail stick in! (3) OK, this is easier said than done, but very quickly with a little practise you will get used to picking up the beads so

lightly on to the cocktail stick that the stickiness of the Goo may pull them off onto the flower without help. Bake in an oven at 250 degrees Fahrenheit that's 120 in Centigrade for 20 minutes. When cool lift the petal parts without the beads on off the tile using a single sided blade. Or you can leave them on through the next baking.

Cut some flower wire (24 or 26 gauge) into pieces of up to 5cm (2"). The length depends on whether you are using the flowers in pots or as cut flowers. For flowers in pots the stem will be shorter.

Professional tip
Here's an interesting idea that seems to work even better on the cheaper non professional version of my stencils because the card hangs on to some of the previous colour when you change colours. To get petals which are lightly bordered with a different colour (for example pink borders on white petals) clean the first colour (pink) from your stencil and then continue to work in white. If you want to experiment with these 'happy accidents' keep changing the colours backwards and forwards. You'll be amazed what you can achieve!

Now dip a piece of flower wire into green Goo and stick into the back of the beads on those flowers with beads. If the fit is snug and the Goo is thick enough the wire should stand up.  If not you'll have to bake them in a piece of Oasis flower foam. Flower foam is OK in the oven at Fimo temperatures

and that will give you a more realistic look to the centre part. I recommend that you look up colours of Gerbera on the internet (images) to make your colour choices. There are lots of fabulous colours but you may find you want some subtle ones as well to enhance bunches with other beautiful flowers as the feature …

but make sure it doesn't touch any elements and that your flowers aren't too close to the elements either.

After this second baking add extra petals by putting a little blob of stiff Goo on the first petal and pressing the second on to it with the back of a cocktail stick or with a ball tool. Bake in between each additional petal set. I put 3 petal shapes together for Gerbera daisies. You can slightly reshape the flowers by pressing them really firmly into some of that squashy dense flower shaping foam (not to be confused with the Oasis flower foam) with a ball tool or the back of your cocktail stick before attaching. It helps to tap the back of the stick or ball tool lightly on some Goo to make it sticky enough to pick the petals up and transfer them to the foam and them to the flower stem.

Note: When pressed into a fairly firm Goo and baked reasonably quickly the 3 dimensional shape (the gap between the petals) is maintained better. Also make sure the petals are arranged so that they fill in the gaps between the lower ones. Finish with a blob of Goo and dip in flower soft, or, alternatively you can use a tiny blob of another colour of clay and texture using a pin or cocktail stick. Press the back of your cocktail stick into the centre

Project 2: Roses

You will need:

Vegetarian pill capsules in size 0 or 00. you can also try other sizes for smaller roses. The smaller sizes have larger numbers For example 000 is really large and size 4 is really tiny. Gelatine capsules do not work as they dry and go brittle in the oven.

To make your own stencils You will need a small craft swivel knife. and thin card or vellum. Photocopy, or trace the pictures of the petals and leaves on page 44 to card. I've grouped into the rose colour and green parts. Cut out the parts to make your stencil. Make sure you leave a couple of centimetres at the bottom of each card. This will be where you hold the stencil to the tile.

You should use a matte tile to reduce the shine, or even a very slightly textured one.

Start with petals. Draw the Goo over the image carefully so you don't catch the little edges. After the first print lift the stencil carefully and place it down again just under the first print. ① Continue printing downwards and then start again at the top. If any of your stencils don't come out well simply scrape away and wipe the tile clean with kitchen roll and start again.

Stencil the petals and centre petal pieces and bake. *(Please note I'm using a stencil from my set).*

Lift the petals using a single sided blade ② then turn them over and add one petal on top of another using a small blob of Goo applied with a cocktail stick. Put the slightly smaller petal on top of the bigger one. Put a tiny touch of Goo into the bottom of the capsule end. This is just to hold the petals down.

You may need to shorten the capsule to just deep enough so that the edges of the petals come just to, or slightly below the edges of the capsule. ③ This makes it easier to handle. Push the petals into the capsule end ④ and

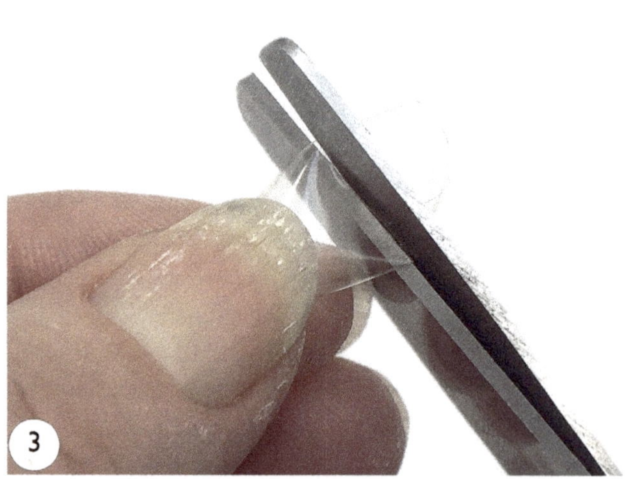

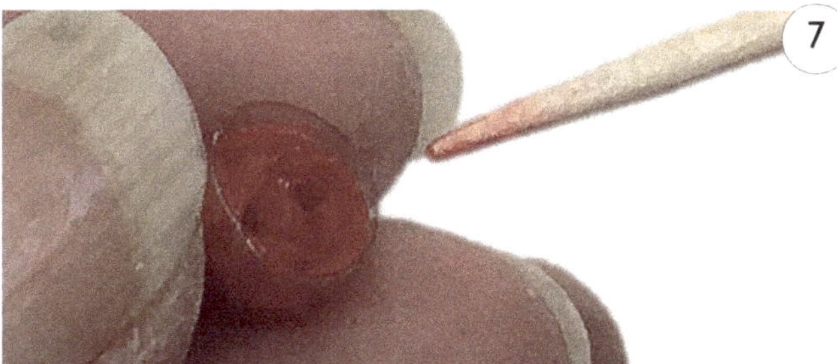

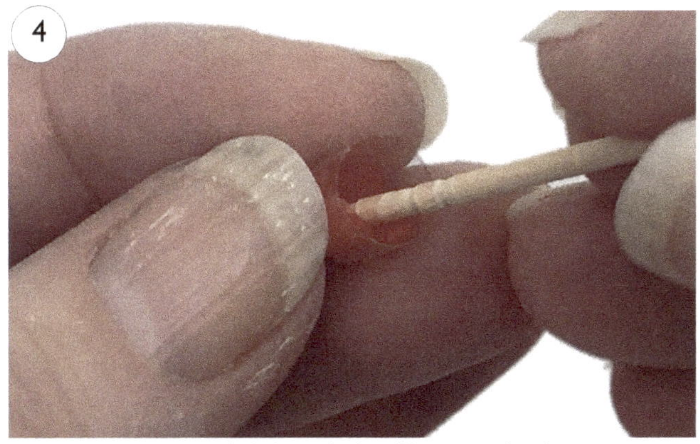

put in an ovenproof dish to bake. You can do the next stage before that bake if you are confident.

Take the long inner petal piece from the tile and wrap it around itself on to the point of a cocktail stick, starting with the narrowest end until you make a small slightly flared cylinder Add a second piece just a little looser. (For a fuller flower you can use more outer or inner petal pieces). ⑤ While the petal piece is still wrapped around the stick, cover the bottom

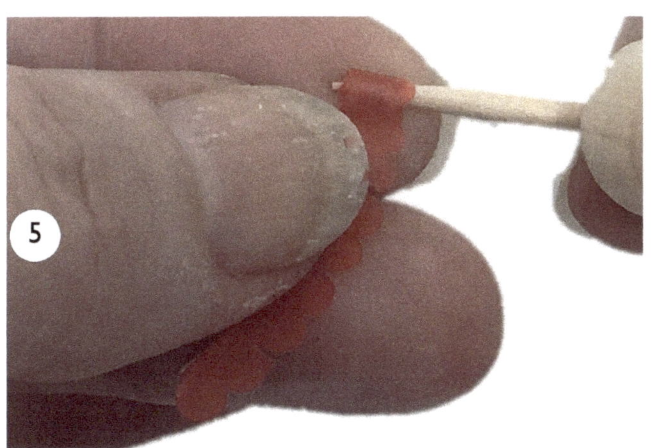

(non scalloped) side with a thick layer of petal coloured Goo and push it all (including the cocktail stick) into the centre of the flower. ⑥ Remove the cocktail stick by a little twist to loosen the hold of the petals. You can hold the petals into the

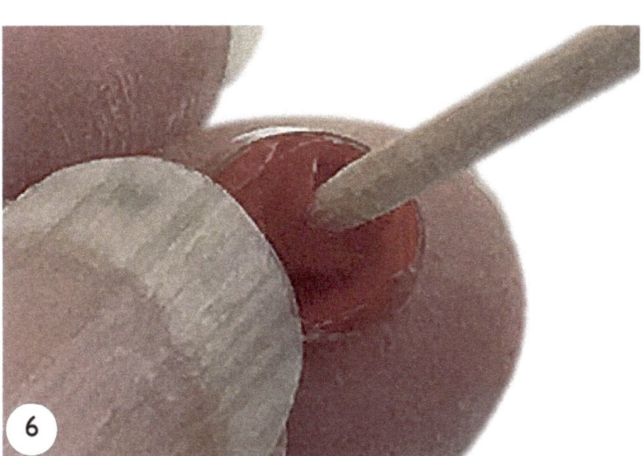

capsule while you do this. ⑦ Put your petals to bake (inside the capsules) in an ovenproof dish

Stencil the calyx, which is the star shape, and the leaf parts in green.

Add a bead to centre of each calyx using a little more Goo, hold a bead on the tip of a cocktail stick. Dip lightly into Goo and place on the calyx. It can take practise to get the pressure just right, so use your fingernail to dislodge from the stick if necessary. Bake.

Remove the calyx from the tile. Using Goo add a long stem about 6+ centimetres long if you want to make a plant,

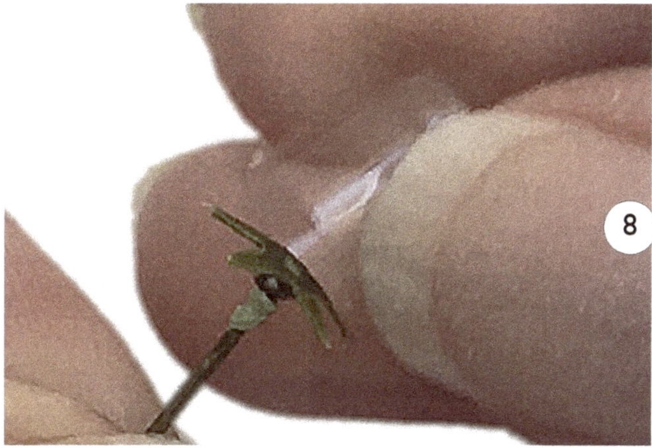

or shorter if you're making flowers for a vase or flower box

Put the stems in some oasis and pop a pill capsule top on each to help the calyx to bend downwards. ⑧

When baked remove the flower heads from the capsule Don't worry about damaging the flower head, it shouldn't be fragile once its baked and cooled. You should be able to release

Professional tip

You can heat this up to help the calyx to bend but you do not need to bake for the full time or at the full temperature. Be aware that baking fully at this stage can break a fragile calyx if you under-baked it the first time because of the heat and pressure of the bending so you either need to bake the calyxes better the first time or leave them to bend inside the capsule without adding more heat at this stage.

it just using your cocktail stick. If the rose does not part from the capsule you may need to split the capsule to release it.

Add very thick Goo to the back of the flower

Press the flower on to the top of a calyx and stem piece. Pop in some Oasis dry flower foam.

Bake again.

You can make very tiny buds by using smaller capsules and just using the inner petals rolled up. In this case you would then dot the calyx lightly with a little more green, or flower

colour push the stem and calyx down through the base of a capsule to hold the calyx against the 'bud' inside the capsule.

Rose leaves

When you have baked your stencilled leaves, turn them over and add a stem by dipping a piece of fine grade flower wire in Goo and simply placing it on the back of the leaf. For sets of 5 leaves add the extra pair below the three (as they appear on my stencils). The home cut ones are singles and pairs because its difficult to make them strong enough in sets. So you will have to assemble these on your wire. Bake The roses can be displayed as they are for a Valentine gift simply tied together with a fine gauzy ribbon or the wires can be twisted together into plants. (9) (10) You can now start playing with colour making the inner petals slightly darker than the outer ones. Mix gradually blending colours by putting a bit of each colour on top of each other on a tile (12) and mix over and over in the same direction to get a really nice blend. Then use different stages of this blend from the outer to the inner petals. (13) Now you're getting arty!

(9)

(10)

(11)

Wrapped Bouqets

To make cellophane wrappers for flower bouquets take small cellophane bags, the lighter weight cellophane the better. Cut a quarter circle from the corner of the bag and snip off the very end of this circle. This makes a perfect posy wrapper. You can use the rest of the cellophane to wrap different size posies and single roses etc. My favourite ribbon for this kind of posy is very fine organza ribbon. Because its very delicate it doesn't detract from the flowers and is good for scale because it looks like a wider mesh ribbon rather like hessian style ribbon.

Project 3: Sunflowers

You will need:

Green flower wire, from size 24 or even thicker in a light green. Mid green Goo for assembling the leaves and yellow for the flowers. Cocktail sticks for dipping in the Goo. Small holed beads in a neutral or pale green colour, the matte ones are best. You will also need brown polymer clay or scenic material or Flower Soft in brown and maybe also some in green or green/brown mix.

The sunflower is a complicated project but a lot of fun to make. The most important thing to remember is to get the yellow colour right. Look at pictures on the internet.

First you will need to make the back of the flower head and the stem with the leaves.

Thickly stencil some green flower backs using the smallest of the flower stencils and spreading a generous layer of Goo over the stencil. That is to say, don't scrape too much of the Goo back off the stencil so that it leaves a generous thickness on the tile when you lift the stencil. Add a small bead to the centre of this green flower back. If necessary build up some extra green Goo around the bead to hold it really securely in place and bake.

Add a long piece (around 6cm) of flower wire bent at 90 degrees at the very end. Add even more Goo to hold it all together. In the same baking, bake your stencilled leaf pairs.

Lift your sunflower leaves from the tile they were baked on and add, matte side downwards over the stems using Goo to attach. Note that the stems should be lying fairly flat on the

tile. This may mean that you press the wire further down at the head end. The flower back should be face down on the tile.

Add two or three sets of leaves and bake.

Professional tip

Be aware that multiple baking can affect light colours like yellow so try to minimise the number of times and length of time you bake. You have to balance this with the fact that under-baking can result in fragile petals.

Making the Flowers

You can also bake these in the same oven as either of the above steps. You will need 3 or more of the petal pieces in either the same size or varying in sizes from large to small for each flower head. Make sure you mix a really good deep golden yellow as a weak yellow won't look right.

Add extra petals to a base petal piece using a thick blob of yellow Goo to glue. Each time press in the middle to stick. This also helps make a natural indentation in the middle. Finish with a blob of brown clay and texture it with a pointed tool. Or you can use flower soft, or home made scenic material see page 24. If you are feeling very artistic you can add various shades in concentric rings. Bake the petal parts on the same tile. Then lift the petal part and Goo to the stem. Bake again.

A picture from my
The Miniature Gardens Book
incorporating several stencilled plants.

Project 4: Tulips

You will need:

Small capsules, usually size 3. These can be pretty hard to get hold of in Europe. See suppliers in the back of this book.

In addition to green Goo and petal coloured Goo you will also need a very light green.

For the colour tricks you need both yellow and red for the petals.

Tulips come in a huge variety of colours including my favourites which look like they've been splashed with red paint. So now we can have some more fun with colours. Mix up a yellow and a red and draw strings of red over the holes in the stencil. ① Alternatively you can just out a dot in the middle as it will smear a little anyway. Add the yellow in the normal stencilling method and you should get some nice irregular smearing. ② ③ Bake them. The tulips are made in a very similar way to the roses except there are no interior petals. Also we add the wire directly into and through the capsule as tulips don't have a calyx. To do this you first need to stick the petals together in pairs or 3s in the same way as you did with the roses ④ and you then push them into the cut down capsules. ⑤ ⑥

You don't need to put any Goo in first to hold them into the capsule. In fact its better if you don't.

Next cut a length of flower wire diagonally to approx 4cm (1½ in). It's important to cut to a sharp point. If you forget and have to re-cut please make sure that any small shards of wire are collected up to avoid any accidental injuries getting them into your carpets and then into feet and little paws etc.

Press the pointed end of the flower wire into and right

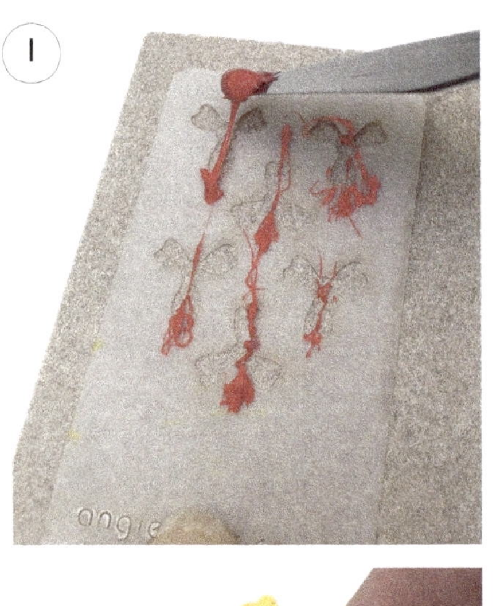

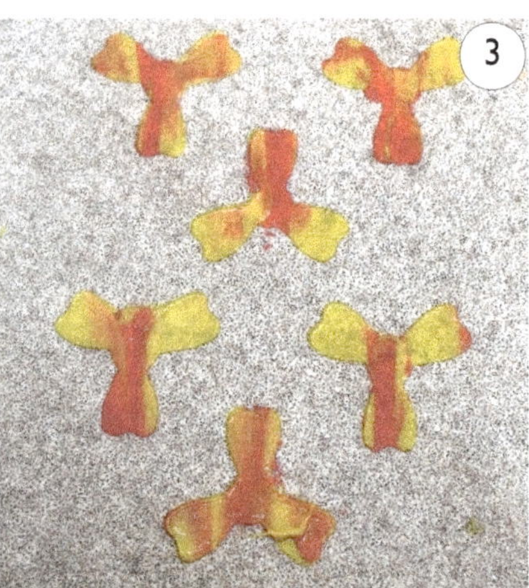

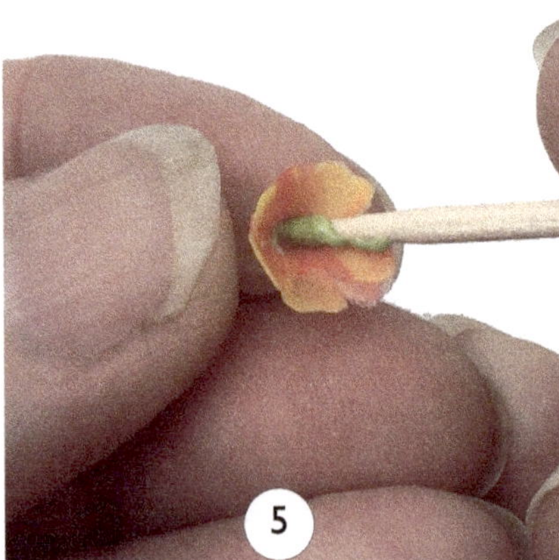

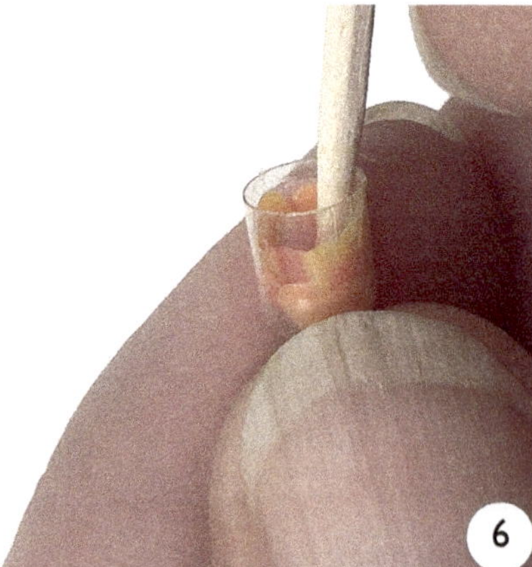

through the petals and the base of the capsule. 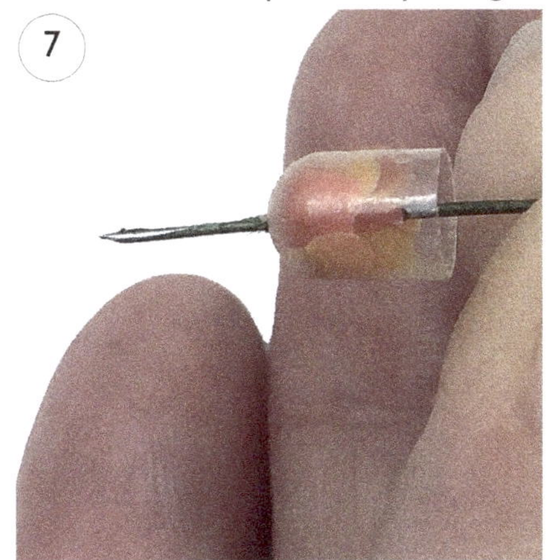 **7** Before pulling right through, dip around a half cm of the top end in light green Goo **8** **9** and pull gently and carefully down until this tip sits very close to the bottom. In other words the Goo needs to start to scrape off the flower wire and glue the wire to the base of the petals. The flowers can then be placed in some dry oasis ready to be baked.

Stencil some of the leaf pairs. These can be baked at the same time as the flowers.

When the flowers and leaves are baked you can remove the flowers from the capsules. Depending on what the capsules are made of they may be easy or difficult to remove. Sometimes you can remove them by simply pushing the stem upwards. Sometimes the capsules may need to be cut away. The larger capsules that I buy in Europe seem to be made of a more flexible material and I haven't yet found smaller capsules that react quite as well. If the centre isn't glued very well the stem may simply push back through. Getting these right does take some practise but the results are so cute its well worth trying again if you don't succeed straight away.

When you have removed the flowers from the capsules you can attach a leaf pair to each flower with Goo and bake again.

7

8

9

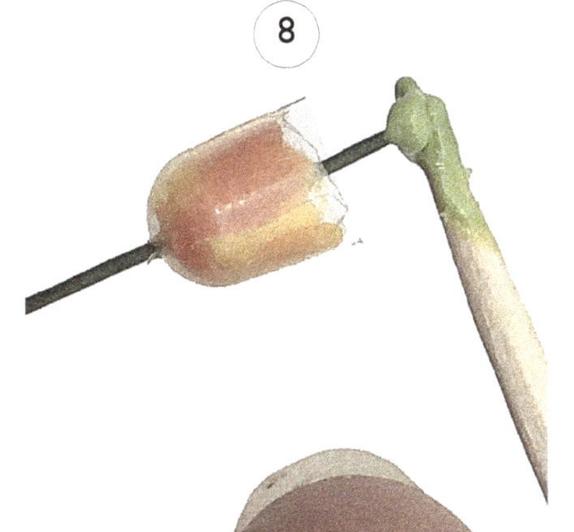

Red and yellow tulips

Some interesting 'smearing' colouring.

When you want to make just the centre part of a flower petal a different colour, dot some colour into the centre of the stencil before overlaying with a different colour. You can experiment but do remember to exaggerate this colour or make it especially thick in comparison with the overlay. This is because it is going to move under the spatula I squeegee and you want to minimise the drag into just one of the petals.

Stop wasting old mixed clay!!!

Home made recycled Polymer clay Scenic crumb and Scenic dust.

You will need:

An electric coffee grinder (or a larger food processing material that can reduce solids to crumb)
2 sieves, one fine and one fairly large.
A face mask so you aren't inhaling any dust
a couple of trays and some ovenproof dishes.

I'm very excited by this new idea because I have so many kilos of colour mixes that just can't be reused for one reason or another. AND it works for all clays. Now I don't have to buy any more scenic materials for my flower centres, for the topiary or for any other mixed media projects I have involving Polymer clay.

Method

Select the leftover clays you want to process and break them up by hand or with a long blade. Or, if you use a machine to mix blitz to a large crumb.

Empty your materials onto an oven proof dish and bake at 100 -110 degrees for just 5 minutes. If you are using a toaster oven set to your lowest possible temp and bake under foil. Remember we want the clay to dry and harden a little but NOT polymerise.

NB * If you bake too long or at too high a temperature, either the material will not cut down at all, or it will take significantly longer to process.

After this first bake return the material to the grinder/ food processor and blitz for a few minutes. Make sure you are wearing a mask and that there are no children/animals around to inhale any dust

Then: take your material outside into the open air if you have a garden or do in front of the window if not. First pass the crumb through the finest sieve, on to a tray. Tap the sieve lightly with your other hand to help the finest dust to pass through.

When all the fine dust has passed through the fine sieve, tip the remainder into the coarser sieve over another tray. This will release the coarser crumb.

Any remaining material which doesn't pass through either sieve can either be blitzed again or you can choose to use it as a coarser material in other projects.

N.B. Your finished and graded materials then need to be re-baked at full temperature. If its all one type of clay bake according to the manufacturers instructions. If its a mix

you may need to raise the temperature towards the higher recommendation.

You can then store your materials for later use in grip bags or recommended plastic tubs.

The Blue Bottle Tree website has an excellent guide to which plastics can be used for polymer clay.

This material can be stuck to regular clay using liquid polymer or Goo and re baked, or you can stick using PVA glue depending on the strength of the bond you want. Once again Blue Bottle Tree do very good information on glues you can use with PC.

The very fine material can be used in place of fine scenic materials and fine flower soft. The medium crumb can be used in place of ordinary flower soft and coarser scenic materials and the left over large crumb is a great large space

scenic material or a base for finer materials. Don't forget to experiment with multicoloured mixes. I've made several of my mixes without pre mixing the clay because I like the variations in colour. Especially in greens which look more realistic when they vary.

NB there is some concern about how many fine particles of plastics get into the environment. Of course this is concern but this is re-using plastic waste that may otherwise be thrown away and so any detrimental effects are balanced somewhat by these positives. We aren't talking about single use plastics here we are talking about art materials. Not many people would suggest that artists don't use oil paints for example and they are a type of air curing 'plastic'.

A brown version of this material can be used for soil and a pale purple for the flowers in the following lavender project:.

Project 5: Lavender Pot

To make a lavender leaf stem you'll need 2 colours of Goo. Dark green and white on a spare tile which you use as a palette. From now on when you're doing some of the advanced multicolour stencils you will get used to using a 'palette' like this. This trick works best if the white is slightly thicker than the green. First stencil the green and make sure you scrape it pretty closely.  You don't want any excess Goo hanging around. Leaving the stencil in place clean your spatula off against the tile you are using as a palette and then scrape white straight over the top. Some of your colour will mix so you will end up with some mixed colour. Scrape this back off your spatula too. You do this by simply pressing firmly and slightly diagonally away from you and dragging the spatula towards you. This mixed colour is not wasted as it's useful for sticking the leaf stems on to wire and also attaching the powder to the flower tops. Get used to scraping this up when it gets messy and popping it in a pile in the corner of your tile!

When these are baked you will see that the back of the leaf is whiter and the whole central stem is whiter too and that the leaf is a nice silvery green. Look closely and you'll see that the edges are beautifully defined. You will notice on my stencils that the pairs of leaves are misaligned slightly. That is so your stem looks 'bushier'. Don't worry that it seems flat at this stage because after baking again you can twist the whole thing to make the little leaves stick out in all directions. The flower stems are painted in a similar colour (a mix of dark green and

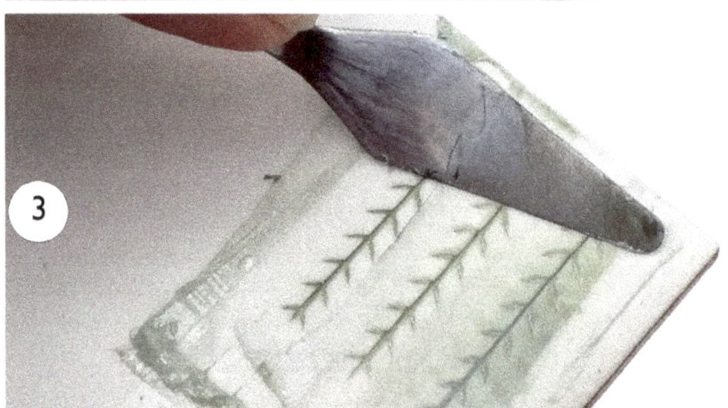

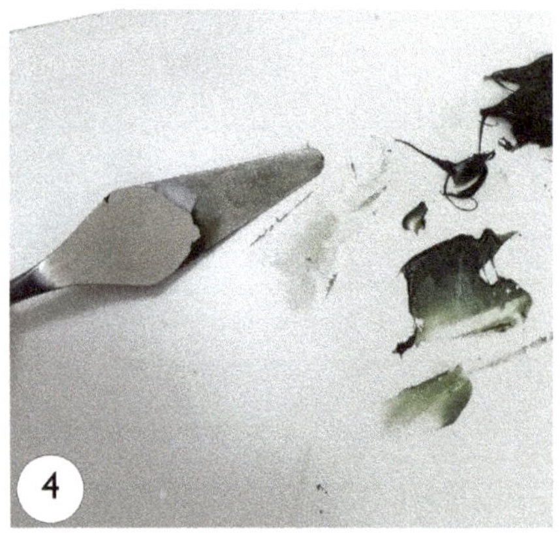

white). Dip them in some Goo and then into some lavender colour crumb. ⑥ See the project for making this at home on page 24, bake these again of course. You can then twist the leaves and flowers together and 'plant' in a pot (see below).

Ageing a terracotta pot

You will need a terracotta pot, some white watercolour paint or matt acrylic and some leaf green watercolour or matte acrylic paint, a soft watercolour brush and a kitchen towel.

First make a very thin mix of white pint and water and swish it all around the pot. ⑦ If you want your pot to display empty swish around the inside too. Don't be too careful about this as if it comes out uneven that can actually be a good thing. You can do second swish around just at the base and turn upside down to dry a little. This will help the particles of paint to droop and dry at a certain level which does loo like the efflorescence of salts coming out of the terracotta part way up.

Then add a little thinned out (but not as thin as the white) green, just on one side and maybe also right round the edge of the base. ⑧ ⑨ This will look like a build up of algae on the side of the pot which is away from the sun and at the base where its most often damp. You can use your fingers or a paper towel to pat some of this paint off if the edge is too sharp.

Filling a pot ready for planting.

First, using old polymer clay of any colour, fill your pot until its a few millimetres under the rim. ⑩ Then smear green or brown Goo right over this filling using a spatula. ⑪ Dip the top of the pot into some brown scenic material or you can use white sand/grit for houseplants. ⑫ Wipe off any excess material/Goo and pat down the surface using a piece of kitchen towel. Finally poke a hole into the centre of the pot with a cocktail stick. Bear in mind if your plant will have a wide stem you may need to wiggle the stick to make it large enough. Bake the whole pot in the oven at polymer clay temperatures.

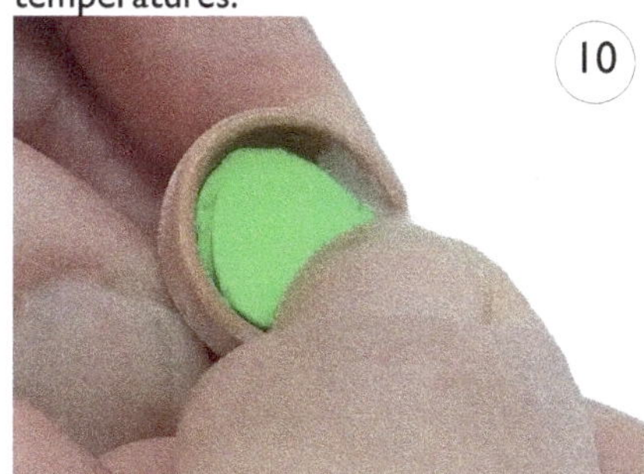

⑩

⑪

⑨

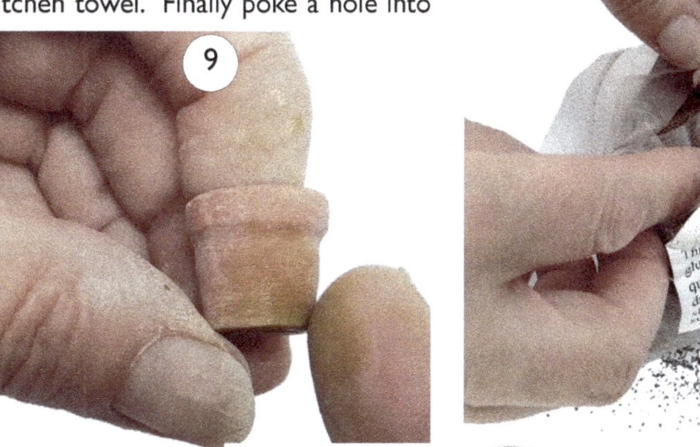

⑫

⑦

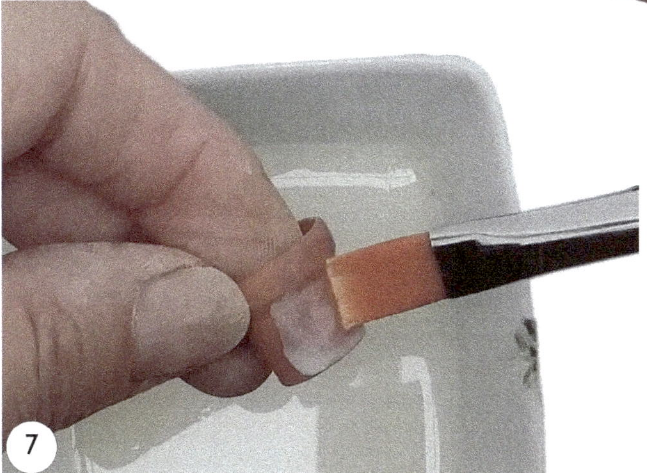

⑧

Project 6 multiple tiny flower plants
Lilac, Hydrangea

You will need:

All the Goo colours, flower wire ball tools cocktail sticks dense EVA type flower foam and dry oasis etc.

You also need some Sculpey mould maker or well conditioned translucent clay. (I used Pro sculpt pale flesh colour which held on the wire very well).

Small flower petals from the multiple blossoms pack or from the individual flower packs.

Some of the most popular plants in the miniature world are some of the most tricky and time consuming because they involve a lot of painstaking fixing of flowers to stems. And each flower needs shaping. There is no absolute shortcut to this but I believe this method is a little bit quicker than most because your petals are the colour you want them to start off with and there's no punching out, just stencilling as many flowers as you want in whatever colour you want.

Professional tip

Take great care when mixing colours. I have seen some otherwise perfect hydrangeas which were a turquoise blue. While there are many different colours of hydrangea, turquoise is not one of them. Take a look at the different colours on Google images and mix to those colours. Don't just guess. You will more than likely be wrong. I have made so many mistakes when mixing colours from memory I just don't do it any more. Make sure you get your lilac colour right. Although there are several colour ways, generally lilacs are slightly pinker than lavender.

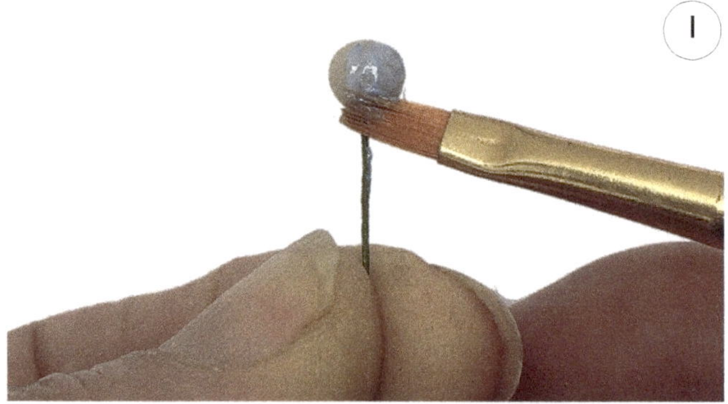

Hydrangea

Take a small piece of Sculpey mould maker and form it on to the end of some flower wire. Form it into a tiny ball and push it on to the end of a flower wire.  If you make a tiny loop in the flower wire it holds on better. Paint this over with a small quantity of Goo in the same colour as the flower petals or a very slightly darker tone of the same colour. The flowers are the wide almost square 4 petal flower. Put a few petals on your flower shaping foam and press firmly with a very small ball tool or a cocktail stick. ② Pick up the petal with a slightly sticky cocktail stick or ball tool and press into the clay where the clay ball meets the flower wire. ③ It should stick well. You can work your way round the bottom edge and then up to

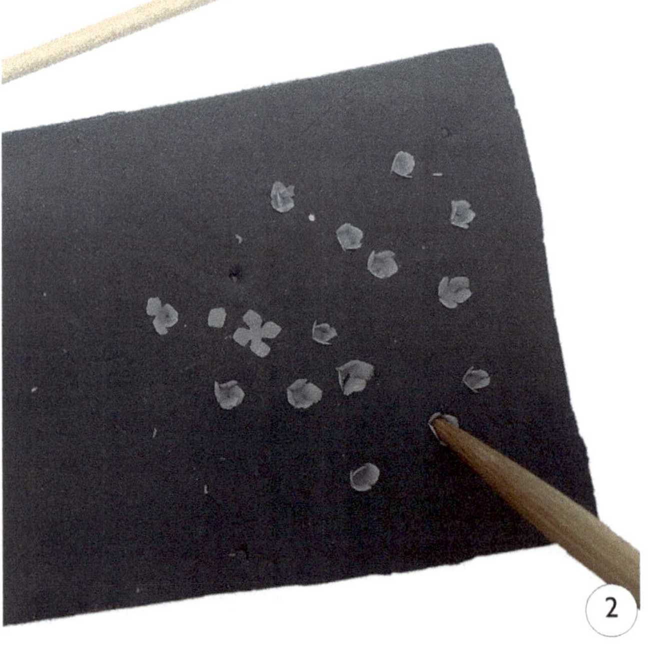

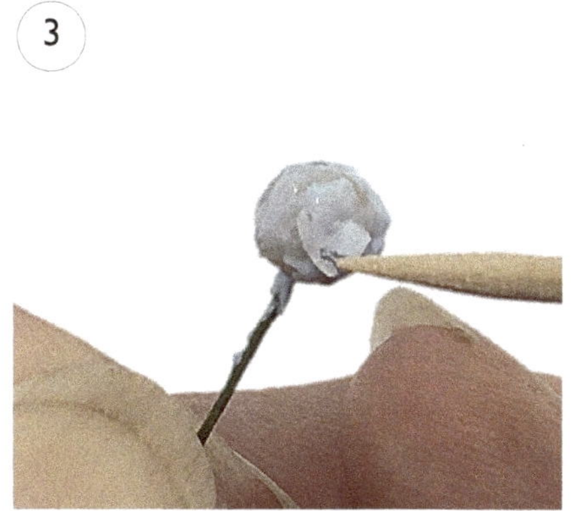

the top of the ball. ⁴ As you press the flower parts down the petals should be pushed up against each other keeping those petal sticking outward. ⁵

Lilacs

To be brutally honest its not really possible to make lilac flowers quite as tiny as we really want them so we have to bodge it. You can simply dip the stems in some scenic material of the right colour as we do with the lavender, however if you are prepared to take a few liberties with scale, the results can be beautiful.

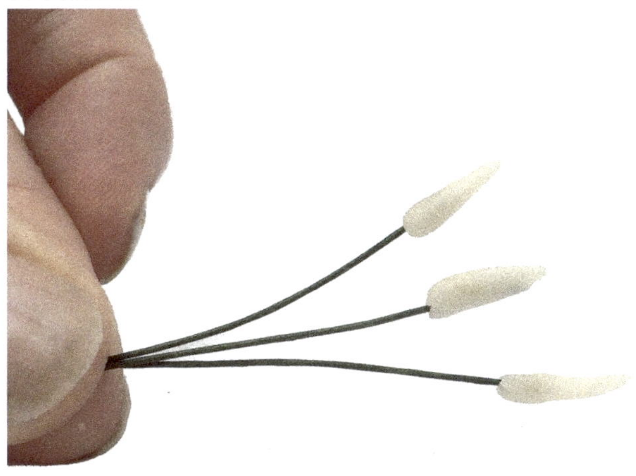

Take a small piece of Sculpey mould maker and form it on to the end of some flower wire. It should be pointed like a tiny carrot but very slightly bent.

This time work backwards from a single flower at the tip, adding more petals as you go.

Bake each little pointed flower bract and wire them together in groups of three along with a few lilac leaves.

Geraniums etc.

Geraniums have many different shapes of flower from the simple red and pink open flowers that we all know to the bunches of tiny rose like flowers. You can make individual flowers on very fine wire and bunch. Or use a small ball or half ball like the hydrangea method.

The tiny blossoms in the blossom pack can also be used to make many small blossom plants including little cherry trees in full bloom before the leaves appear. Use a dried plant and coat with brown Goo and simply stick blossoms all over them. Other ideas for small trees and bushes are in my The Miniature Gardens Book

Project 7: wiring techniques for shrubby plants rose bushes etc.

You will need:

A thick mix of Goo in the stem colour of the plant you are building. In this case I've used a mix of Premo alizarin crimson and Fimo terracotta both mixed into a thick Goo with Liquid Fimo.

Acer

The plant shown in the project is made with inner leaf stencil from variegated coleus. For a different leaf shape you can use the acer/cannabis stencil.

I originally found this idea from the wonderful Mary Kinloch who works with paper flowers has a video (**www.youtube. com/watch?v=BA4aPxcmiJk**) showing her technique for gluing various leaves together on to one stem. Basically she bends each leaf ① and attaches them on to the main stem

to be a form of instant bonding glue.

This technique can also work with Goo as long as it is thick enough and you don't try to do right round the plant at one time. Work on one side and bake. ② Then twist and arrange the leaves to suit. If your Goo is thick enough you can add extra leaves at any point up to the final bake.

My other technique for wiring isn't as pretty as Mary's. Its useful for climbing roses and tomato plants etc. Its just a matter of grabbing two or more wires at a time. Arranging them so they stand at different levels and twisting firmly to lock them together. ③ ④ Then putting several of these together to make a plant. If the wires aren't thin enough this can result in an unsightly jumble of wires which is difficult to disguise but you can do a couple of things to minimise this. Firstly you can cut

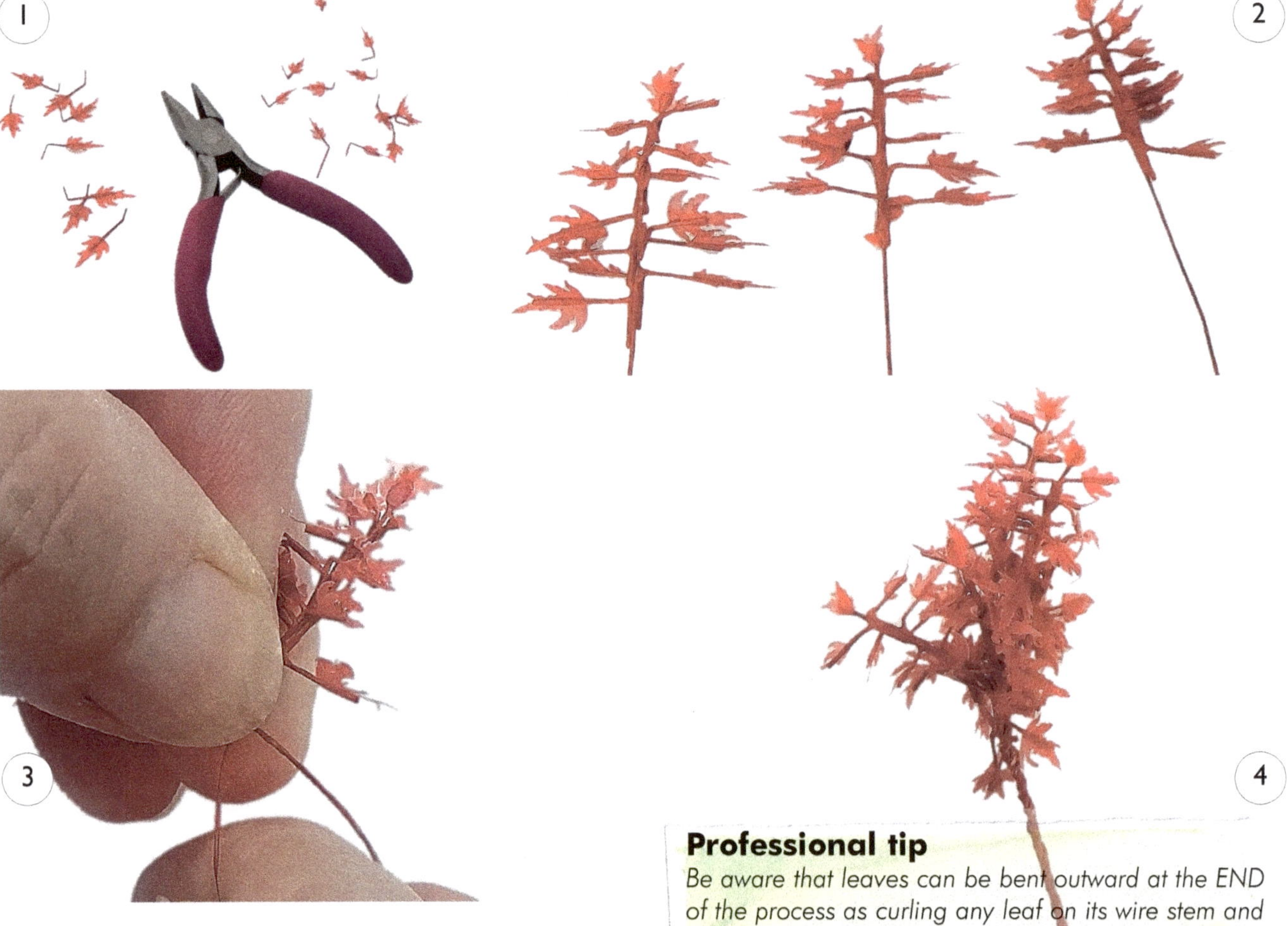

with a mixture of white glue and something called zap-a-gap which I don't believe is available in Europe but which seems

Professional tip

Be aware that leaves can be bent outward at the END of the process as curling any leaf on its wire stem and then baking afterwards can result in cracking when heat and pressure work together on clay.

out some of the wires once they are firmly twisted in and then you can 'lock' the wires by adding a little Goo and baking. You can also paint on more Goo to disguise the twisty wires. ⑤ Of course it then always has to be baked again. Or you can go back to Mary's non-bake method using glue and paint mix to disguise.

Twiggy things

Sometimes you need a bit of height or a bit of hang on your plant displays. For that reason I designed the stencil pack I call "twiggy things". It consists of a twiggy shape and some flowers and leaves. If you want you can just use twigs stencilled in green, or various shades of brown . You can wire the twigs for upright displays or just let them hang for hanging baskets. To add leaves or blossoms you need to stencil and bake those first and then stencil the twigs over. It doesn't work well if you try to reverse this.

Professional tip
Why stop at green and brown twigs. Why not sprinkle with pearl or glitter powder before baking and remove the excess onto a sheet of paper and back into the jar after. Be aware some glitters are based on plastics and may fuse to your tile. Some interesting effects maybe? Otherwise just remove from your tile with a single sided blade.

Project 8: Lilies & Orchids

You will need:

Green Japanese flower wire and Goo in white for this colour of lily (there are also yellow and orange star lilies). A very small amount of light green and some burgundy red colour green for the leaves. Cocktail sticks for dipping in the Goo. Some tweezers, small scissors and some fibre. You can get fine fibre in railway modelling shops. In this picture I'm using the fibre from a mature globe artichoke but in some of the finished ones I've used a variety of other fibres. You also need a stiff brush. The one I'm using is called a foliator but a cheap stiff brush will do the trick.

Star Lily

Stencil the petals (you will use 2 petal parts for each flower) and bake. I've chosen white star lilies which are my favourite. I have just coloured them very simply but you can decide how much patience you spend on painting them. You could also use indelible ink colouring pens for colouring onto Polymer clay. I've chosen to use more Goo and simply using a stiff brush stipple the deep red Goo on to the petals. (1) Some will also land on the tile but this isn't a problem. I then added green in the centres of the petals. (2) I've done this really quickly and you can build these colours up more slowly baking in between layers in which case you could add a pink layer too. Or you can use a colouring pen with permanent ink to add the colours.

Making Flowers

(with or without leaves see professional tip for making the stems with leaves first.)

Cut some flower wire into pieces of 5cm / 2". You will need 2 of the petal pieces for each flower.

Put a pair of petals together using white Goo to glue them together. You can encourage the petals to shape a little by pressing firmly onto a flower mat with a ball tool. If you don't have a flower mat any craft foam will do. Thick Goo is good for gluing the petals on because the pressure in the centre naturally forces the Goo outwards, thus providing support to the new shape of the petals, making them stick forward a little. If I'm making white or pink lilies I use a very light green Goo

as it shows through and looks natural. Poke a piece of wire through the petal pair. You may find it easiest if you use a needle tool to poke the hole in to the petals first. Feed the wire through until there's just 1cm or less showing and put a tiny blob of pale green Goo on the stem before pulling it back a little further to bed it in to the centre of the flower. ③ Press in some very short pieces of light green scenic grass or fibre to simulate the stamens. ④ Bake again. If you take the flowers out hot you can hold the flowers together to help them cool into a natural shape.

Orchid

Once again you can stencil and then overlay the pre-baked petals with a contrasting colour. This time I'm not spotting but rather dragging the colour. ⑤ You also need to stencil the little centre bits in the contrast colour. Add tiny pearl or white no hole beads in the top centre of this tiny part before baking so that it sticks well. ⑥ You will find it helpful to dip a cocktail stick into

a little liquid polymer before picking up the beads with the sticky end of the cocktail stick and depositing them one by one on the central bits to simulate the 'column' (plant etymology). I mean that little blobby bit in the middle!

When all the parts are baked and coloured you can encourage the petals to shape a little by pressing firmly onto the back of each petal on a flower mat with a ball tool. If you don't have a flower mat any craft foam will do. Place the first 3 petal piece triangle point up and add the second part with the two petals pointing sideways (slightly upwards). Thick Goo is good for gluing the petals on because the pressure in the centre naturally forces the Goo outwards, thus providing support to the new shape of the petals, making them stick forward a little. If I'm making white or pink orchids I use a very light green Goo as it shows through and looks natural. Add a tiny blob of Goo to the centre of the flower and add the third shape. The widest part, with the bead on, sticks to the centre.

You can bake these at this point to make them easier to use later.

Cut some flower wire into pieces of 5cm / 2". Dip the tip of each piece into Goo of the same colour as the petals or in a light green and support in flower foam to bake. This is to form an immature flower tip. After baking curve this stem and you can bend the tip to face down if you like. You can then add mature flowers to just one side of the stem using Goo before baking again. In

the case of this flower I don't add any extra wire to the backs of each flower, simply add them directly to the main curved stem but if you want more distance from the stem you can add a bead to the back of the flowers. It is best to use both sizes of the flower provided in the pack.

Leaves

Wiring leaves: Cut some flower wire into pieces of 2.5cm (1"). Poke the tip of each wire deeply into the green Goo, press on one side side of the leaf leaving just a very small tip showing beyond the leaf and re bake.

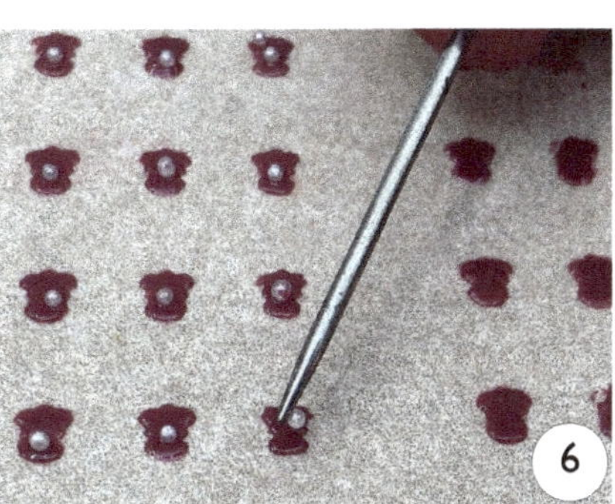

Project 9: 2 & 3 stage stencilling
Spider plants and other variegated plants

Spider Plants

In addition to the obvious colours and stencils you will need you should also mix a little very light green in a fairly thick mix. This is to help the babies 'grab' on to the stems.

Two stage stencilling allows you to make variegated leaves simply and quickly. I just love the way these look and although on the pack I put the difficulty level at 3, really I find them so easy to make!

For these plants its not so easy to make your own stencils so I'm going to suggest that you get mine as we've put the work into making sure they line up. You still need to use your eyes and be careful to line them up perfectly.

Simply take the smallest (thinnest) of the big pair of leaves and the smallest of the small pair. These are the inner part of the leaves.

Print in your first colour choice, usually either white or green. ① Some spider plants are a purple/pink colour. Look at photos online. The larger set is for the main plant and

the smaller set is for the 'babies'. Bake your first stencilling. When your tile has cooled, overlay the second stencil using the locator points (which look like little flowers) to guide you and stencil in your other chosen colour over the top of the first leaves. ②

You will find that mostly the first colour will show through, as the second colour falls to the side of it. Don't worry if its not perfect as the other side will be clearer. Bake your second set of stencilled work. Remove your stencils from the tile when cooled using a single sided blade. The large leaves can be 'planted' directly into a filled plant pot using a cocktail stick and Aleene's tacky glue (or similar). [3] Make sure you use this tool to leave space in the middle for some flower wires for the baby plants.

To make the spider 'babies'

Stencil in the same way as the main plant and bake. Add one two or three sets of three leaves to a piece of flower wire (formed into a curve) dipped in thick Goo. The leaves should be pointed upwards. It is important that your Goo is very thick for this job otherwise the leaves will fall off the flower wire. If your Goo is not thick enough you can leave a bit on some plain paper for a while to remove some of the moisture and oils. I advise you to use a very light green colour which you can mix from your original colours. You can use a plant pot to hold these curved wires while baking or tiny pegs as shown. [4] Add these stems to the middle of the plant pot using tacky glue.

Variegated leaves

You will need green white and yellow Goo

Ivy

We've produced an ivy set where the various shapes and sizes of ivy leaf actually 'nest' in each other for printing. This means you can either stencil each separately, as plain single

colour leaves. Or you can choose any two out of the set to produce variegated leaves using the above technique of double baking. Alternatively you can choose not to bake between colours and produce a slightly smeared effect which can be very subtle and 'painterly'.

Variegated Ivy

Firstly you need to turn your tiles round if they are rec-tangular so that your lines of stencils are as long as possible.

This is because you may want to put a second colour over the first without even baking the first one. If you stencilled the whole tile with the first colour and then started working on the second colour you would end up making a real mess!

You start with a smaller size of leaf. We've designed this set so that they nest. You can therefore use any combination of two (or even 3 if you're really adventurous) leaf shapes.

Stencil a line of the smaller size either in a light or dark green. Then switch to the stencil with the larger sized leaf and line up over the first set so that the smaller leaf is entirely within the larger one but the stem end is almost touching the first colour. Stencil the second colour over the first. Then you can start again on the next line.

If you want a sharper definition you can stencil and bake the first colour before adding the second. You have to make sure that your first colour is cleanly stencilled and not lumpy and sticky in both methods.

Hostas

Now we get on to some really lovely multiple stencil techniques. I started looking at the possibilities of making leaf veins. These are pretty tricky stencils to design but not as hard as it may seem to use, especially if you already have some stencilling experience. Previously we've used the smallest stencil first followed by the bigger stencil but in this case the leaf vein is bigger than the second stencil. This doesn't cause as many problems as you would expect because the veins themselves are pretty good at holding on to the next layer of colour. So lets get straight into the method and you'll see what I mean.

Firstly you need to turn your tiles round if they are rectangular. Just as you did with the Ivy If you did that one first. The reason for this is that when you put a second wet colour on you don't want to be working over a lower layer of the first one. You will get this wrong at some time … I did!

First stencil the leaf veins in a very pale green, ^① horizontally along the longest length of your tile if your tile is rectangular. Fill your tile and bake the first imprint. Decide whether you are making a variegated hosta leaf or just a plain colour. If you're making a plain colour you can move straight on to the large leaf shape and stencil that in mid or dark green or there are other colours (look up Hosta images

If you are doing a variegated hosta your next shape will be the jagged edge leaf shape. Lay that over the leaf veins so that the top curve of the veins is just visible inside the stencil and the middle vein is lined up down the centre. Stencil your second colour. ② In my example I've added a darker green centre. Do an entire line of these but don't step down to the next line. Change colours (in my example to a light yellowy green) and line the whole leaf stencil up over the previous 'print' ③ in exactly the same way making sure all the tips of the 'skeleton' are within the new stencil. You will see that the colour smears a little but this gives a nice painterly effect. Clean your spatula off on the palette tile between each stroke. This helps make sure your colours don't muddy too much.

for inspiration).

When you have finished this line, go back to the first colour and start on the next line.

When your leaves are finished, after baking the wires on, you can take a tiny peg (available in craft stores and import shops), fold the leaf in half and peg the back. ④ ⑤ If you press your finger against the tip of the leaf as you're putting the peg on, you can get a nice little curled down tip. Go on. Try it!

Professional tip

If you want your colours to smear less you can leave the first of the two leaf colours on the tile to soak in a little. This pulls some of the oils out of the Goo and makes it drier. When you then add the second colour the first colour moves, and therefore smears less. In this way you can alter the definition of your variegation subtly.

Project 10: Hanging baskets

I've chosen to make 2 styles of hanging baskets, the traditional half spherical ones and the more modern and currently very popular cone shape.

You will need:

Some masking tape and some twine, the quality of the twine you use will affect the finish of your basket. You also need some quick drying tacky glue and an apron. Be prepared to get your fingers a bit gluey for this project. For the dish shape hanging basket you'll need a ping pong ball. Cheap plastic ones will do or a polystyrene ball.

For the cone shaped basket you'll need 1/3rd of a circle. Or you can photocopy the one on this page on to paper and then press the image through the paper on to Tetrapak card, that's the card that milk and juice cartons are made of.

You will also need jump rings and chain and possibly a hook which you can make at home using fine wire and round pliers. If you have a 3D pen you can use wood filament for a similar result (with practise). You could also make wrought iron style hanging baskets using 3D pen.

The dome shape

For the half spherical ones use string wound and glued round the sphere starting by piercing a small hole in the end of the ball to pop the string through, then add a blob of glue and make your first wind which is the most difficult one. Tape this down with masking tape and walk away until it dries or at least partly dries so that its not always moving about when you do the rest of the winds. Then its simply a matter of trailing

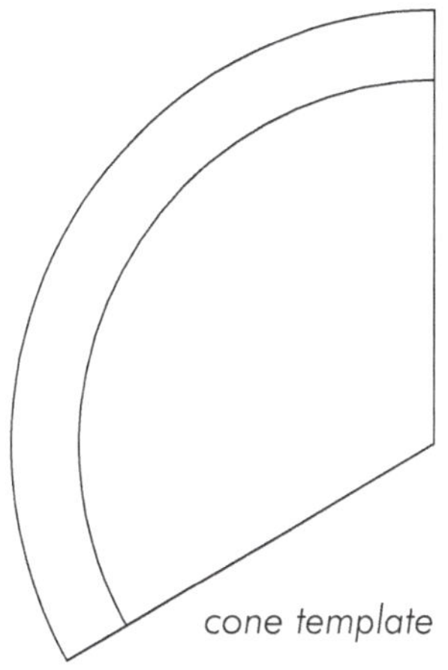

cone template

the glue around and bringing the string up to meet each row. Some glue will leak through but if you aren't afraid to simply wipe it off with a finger it doesn't cause any problems. When you get to the half way point separate the layers of twine (mine had three twists) and cut one off at a time tucking the cut end inside where it will be invisible, then winding a little bit more and cutting the second and then the third. This makes sure the end is gradual and not an ugly lump.

The cone shape.

Start by taping the cone together. You may need to use a craft tool to curve the card a little to stop it simply bending. If you have ever curled ribbon the method for 'curling' card is similar. Start the wind by taping the end piece of the string on to the card vertically next to the join line to help hide it, and begin winding each wind as close as possible to the last. Start at the narrowest point of the cone and glue on a couple of winds first, then stop and tape down to dry. When the first and most difficult wind is dry, continue glueing and winding until you reach the top. Finish in the same way as described in the dish shaped basket. Leave to dry and remove the card. Both types of basket look best with chain supports although you could use the same string to make hangers.

Afterwards you can carve an oasis foam filling to fit, cover all over in soil substitute and push into the basket. Arrange your plants inside.

If you have a 3D pen and want to use it for this project wood filament looks good for the cone shaped hanging basket and black for a wrought iron hanging basket. You may also need wrought ironwork supports (not shown) which you can make in card or once again in 3D pen. If using 3D pen simply transfer the shape to the silver side of some Tetrapak card and draw thickly over the designs. Make both sides and stick together using more filament. If making in card use $1/4$ centimetre depth card strips and make sure to use a knitting needle (the small wooden or bamboo ones are the best) to roll the strips around. Depending on the thickness of card you use you may need a double thickness but remember a second layer will be bigger or smaller than the first depending on whether you put it inside or outside. In my shop I simply added small jewellery loops to the building.

Top tip

Find the line where the two halves of the ball is glued together and make your first hole exactly opposite this. This will help you to make an accurate half globe dish shape. When your basket is dry simply remove the ping pong ball by pressing each side to loosen. You may not be able to use the ball again as it will probably not regain its shape.

Project 11: Topiary

You will need:

Dry (oasis style) flower foam
A butter knife

A piece of rough sandpaper
A face mask
Green Goo

Green scenic scatter, or see page 24 for home made scenic material.

To put in the centre of a lantern shop which has a central tea-light holder a really great idea is to plant a twirly 'topiary' tree. Or you can use them for filler plants at the back of a shop or outside the shop on either side of the door. They are really easy to make but you could also refine them using tiny leaves instead of or in addition to scenic scatter.

Cut a deep triangle from the oasis ① and then start to shave off the edges until you get a cone shape. ②

When your topiary shape is finished you may ned to refine the shape by narrowing the bottom (this stage is not shown). This is so that it fits neatly into your container or pot.

Starting at the top point make a diagonal cut right round the tree to the base. ③ Cut diagonally into this mark in both directions to remove a v shaped groove of the oasis material. Its fun to carve isn't it!

Then start again and cut a second 'twirl'. ④ Roll your sandpaper into a tube and use this to sand the grooves until you have a smooth (use a mask for this process).

Apply a coating of green Goo over the whole surface and then dip in scenic material until it is well coated. (5) Bake in the oven. You can also make topiary using small balls I used polystyrene balls (6) but since there may be fumes this is not recommended in a home or toaster oven. Make sure anything you do make doesn't get too close to any heating element.

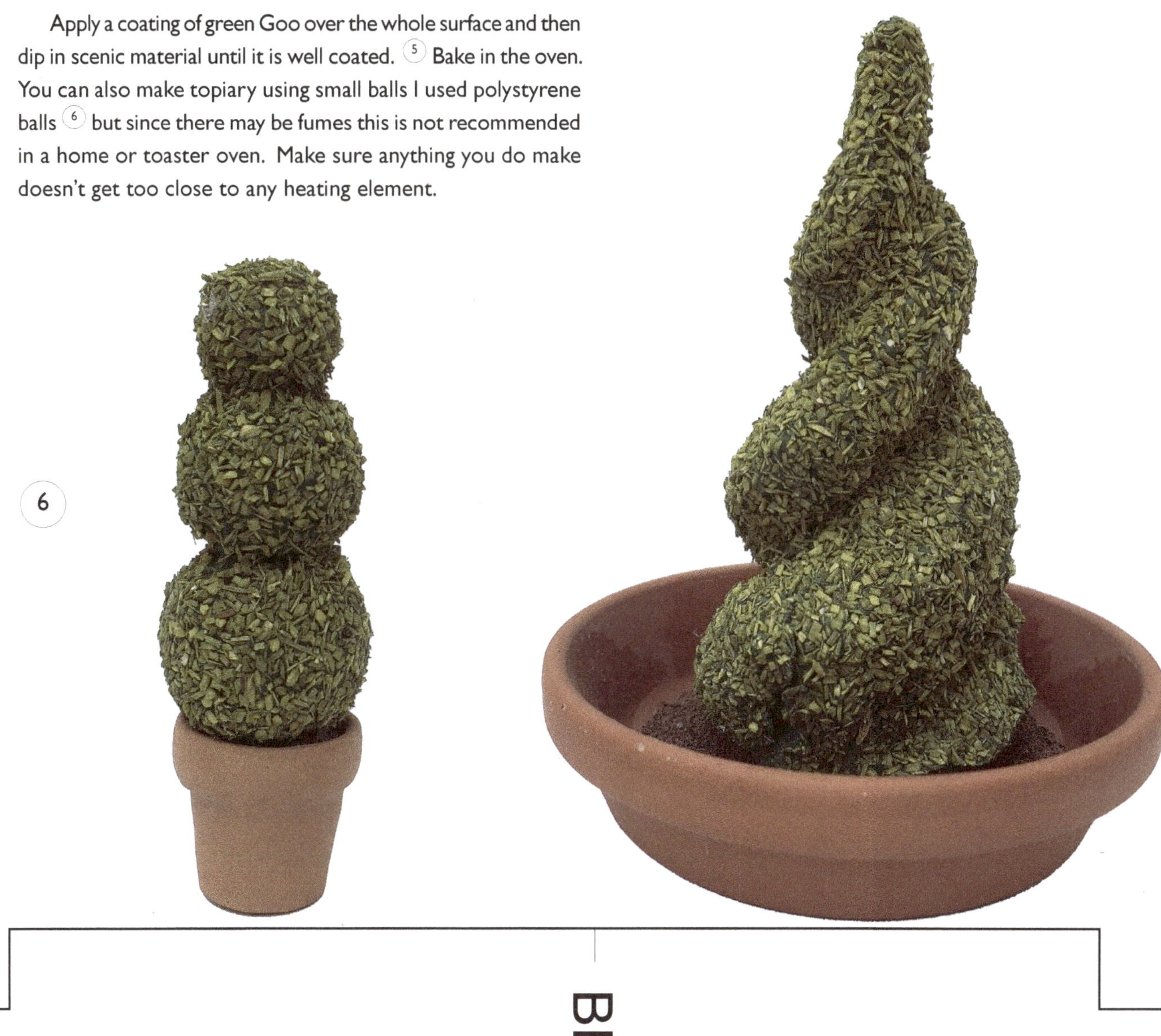

BEND

BOTTOM

TOP

Pattern for internal walls for the IKEA lantern on the next page

Project 12: IKEA lantern

You will need:

The lantern, or similar
Small animal cage wire mesh
Craft wire
Spray paint (to change the wire colour). I used Green.
Scissors that you don't mind being damaged or pliers or wire cutters
A dowel of around 1.5cm diameter (approx. half an inch)
Foamcore or hardboard etc. if you want to raise the floor.

Since this lantern may not always be available I hope you'll see this as a guide on how you can repurpose items like this as miniature flower shops. Ikea also has mini greenhouses for cactus, deep photo display frames etc. and its well worth seeking out interesting display materials and using some of these simple ideas with them.

Cut 2 pieces of wire mesh for the side walls of the lantern. The shape is shown on the previous page. If you are changing the colour spray paint it now. The top extended piece bends into the rectangular ventilation hole under the lid part (shown in the big picture). The bottom lip tucks into the bottom vent and bends right up butt first you will need to bend the whole piece up around half way down before fitting the mesh into its final position.

Make pot and flower tub holders as shown in ① ② ③ ④ using your dowel to wrap a piece of wire around and bend up

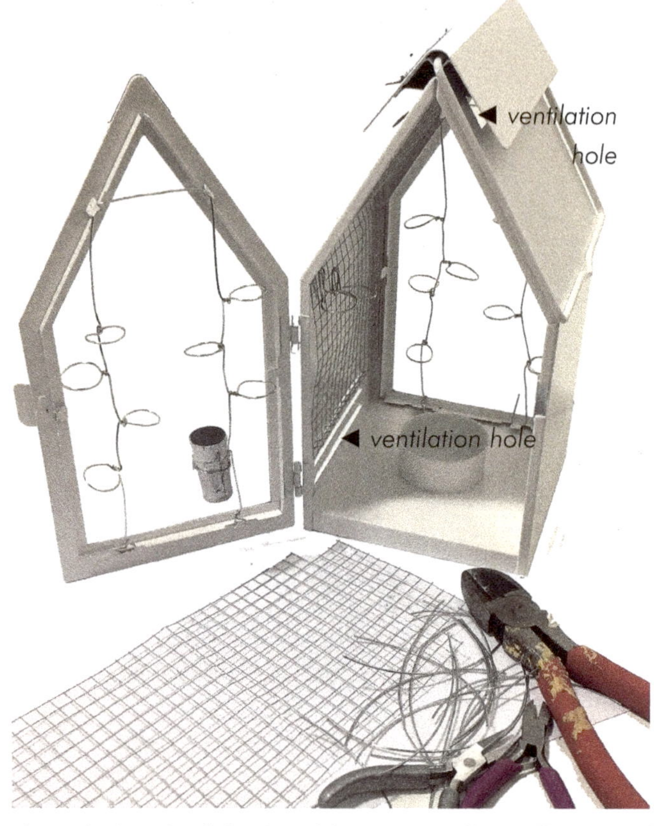

along the length of the dowel leaving a small gap. The size of dowel you use depends on the size of pot you want to hang but for the flower tubs I've used a dowel to wrap the wire around and just left a small gap between the wires to allow me to

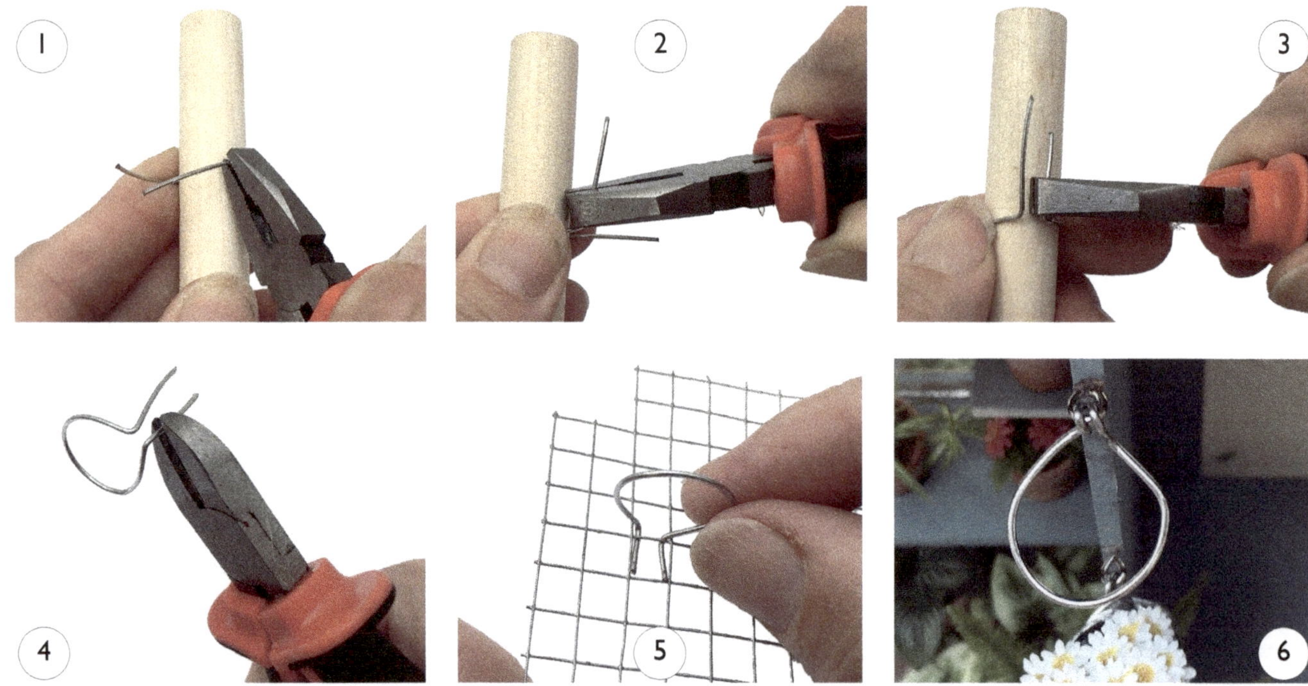

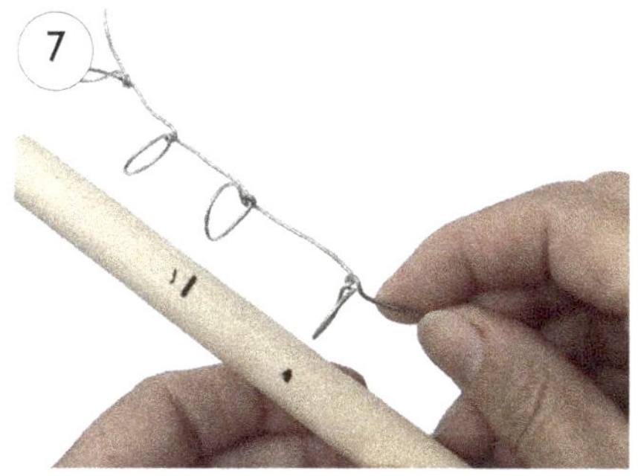

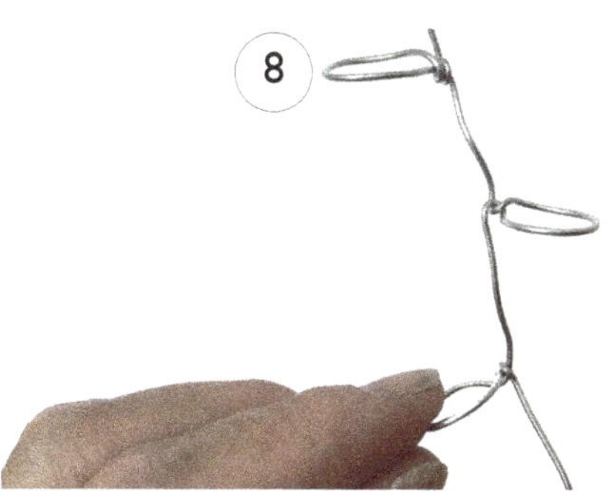

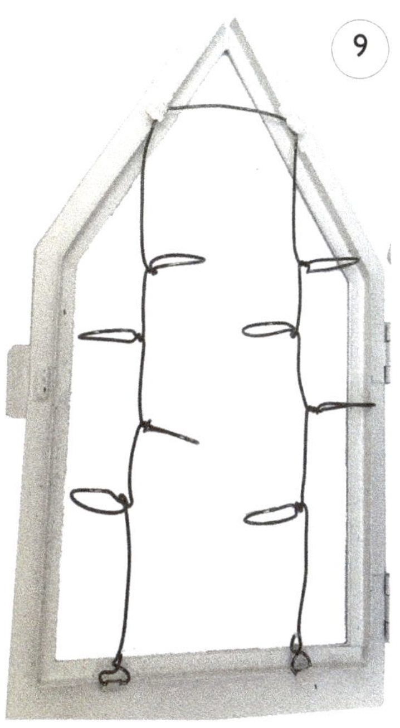

pinch the hooks into the mesh holes. (5) It then springs back a bit into the gap in the mesh. You can also use these holders in a small eyelet as seen on the side of a wooden shop. (6) These eyelets are available at jewellery suppliers. The other long pot holder wires I made by wrapping right round the dowel. Bending and then pulling back off the dowel to twist. (7) I made 2 marks on the dowel to show the distance between the hoops and then I twisted every other hoop to point in the opposite directions. (8) I made a loop on the bottom of the wire and then measured across the glass retainer hooks at the top of the 'doorway' and bent downwards and repeated the process for the second half. I made 2 of these. One for the doorway and one for the back of the 'shop'. Spray paint these too before fitting. As you put the glass back bend your wire over the retainers and make loops at the bottom and hook the loops over the retainers before bending them back into place. (9) *

Cut a piece of Foamcore or hardboard to the measurement of the base of the lantern remembering to account for the space where the door and the pots hanging from the doorway might sit. And the space that the wire walls take up. I measured to just in front of the candler holder. Cut out press the Foamcore on to the tealight holder. Take it back out and cut out the circle if you wish to indent a topiary tree. Or you can leave the holder covered. You will also need to make a step front. You may have to make a back support too. It doesn't need to be 100 percent perfect as hopefully you'll hardly see it for the number of flowers you cram in there!

* IMPORTANT NOTE:

If the lantern is for a child to play with you will need to replace the glass with polycarbonate. Also fill or cover the night light holder so they are not tempted to light any candles in it!

Loosen the glass holders and change the glass if you need to.

Cut your own stencils and kits

Simply photocopy these onto 200gsm card and cut out.

All content (c) copyright and for personal use only, do not resell these patterns.

Flower Tub

1. Curl the large piece A as you would a piece of ribbon. Hold one end and put your forefinger on one side and a small wooden tool or paintbrush on the other side of the card and drag across the length to curl it. Glue the small tab on the end and attach the other side, holding firmly for a few seconds for the glue to grab.

2. Take the circular piece B and bend all the tabs down. Put a line of glue inside A at the narrow end. Insert B with the tabs pointing down. This will be a tight fit, use a wooden tool to help adjust the position. Nip around the edge to help the glue grip.

3. Please note each of the strips C-E has a gentle curve, this should have the arc upwards towards the widest part of A for assembly.

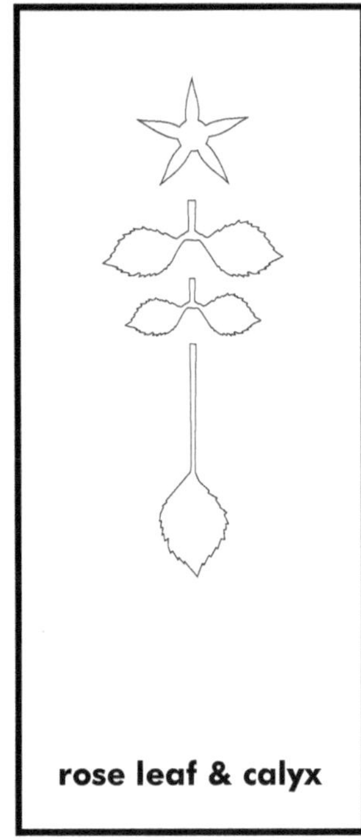
rose leaf & calyx

rose petal & centre

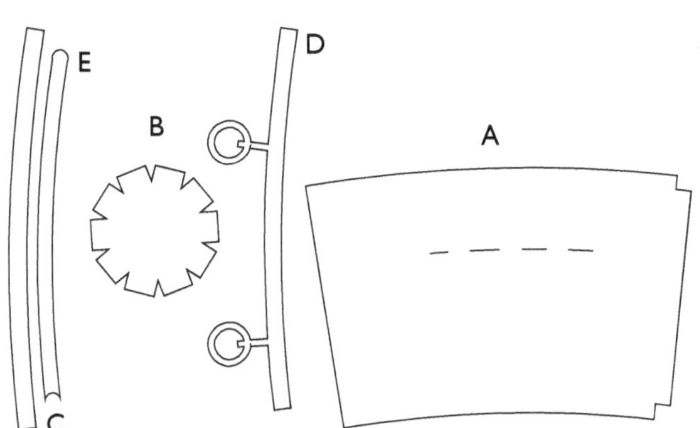

Jug

Assemble the body and base as per the flower tub. The curved piece forms the spout to top of the jug. Curl the longest strip and attach it to the glued tabs of the base inside. Use the wooden tool if necessary. Glue the overlap. Curl and glue the shortest strip around the bottom of the spout. The mid size strip is the handle, curl it and fix to the body at the other side to the spout.

4. Glue a line around the outside of A at the top (widest part). Take piece C (flat ended) and add it, avoid joining at the centre line to strengthen the piece. The join should be perfect with no overlap.

5. Glue a line on the outside of A 2/3rds of the way up where there is a faint scoring. Attach piece D with the handles pointing upwards, clear of the glue. Then turn the loops to point downwards and glue the connecting strips to the main strip of D.

6. Glue a line around the bottom of A and attach piece E (round ended).

7. Spray paint in a small cardboard box to contain the spray.

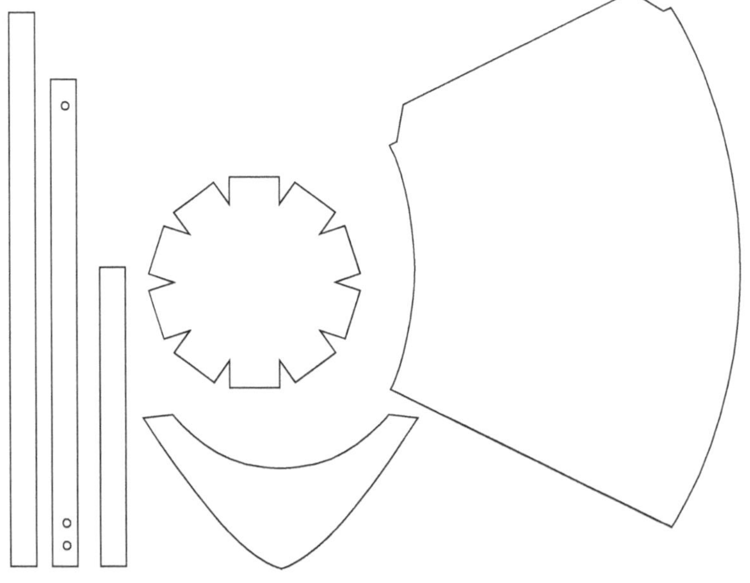

Other things things you can do with stencilled flowers and leaves

You can add them to mini hats and clothes and handbags and shoes either by sewing on. It would be best to use a tiny bead to sew through into and back out of. This protects the flower from being cut by the thread. Or you can glue them on with jewellery glue. You can also fill tubs and trugs and baskets with flowers as permanent displays in mini tea shops etc. Put them in dolls hair or as little posies. Make copies of your friends wedding flowers.

Try spatula applying a thin coat of Goo or a thin coat of translucent Fimo to a tile and simply sticking the flowers to it then you can lift and use as a 'fabric'

You can also cut bits of this flowery 'fabric and apply to greetings cards etc.

Because I believe that stencilled flowers are pretty water-proof you can probably appliqué them to full size clothes hats etc. I haven't tried it yet but I absolutely believe that Goo can be used as a glue for these flowers if you want to add them to cotton tee shirts or cotton fabric. Of course you will have to bake afterwards and I suggest wrapping your fabric lightly in tinfoil to prevent any fabric catching any flame or filament. I wouldn't necessarily suggest machine washing afterwards because I don't know. I have trialled using Liquid Fimo to appliqué my superfine slices onto silk as well so I know that it works although I can't be responsible for any losses incurred by copying the above 'daft ideas!'.

Gallery

List of stencils at time of printing

Acer / Cannabis

Butterfly

Dahlia

Daisy

Dandelions

Gerbera

Grape Leaf

Herbs #1 Parsley, Rocket and Basil

Herbs #2 Mint, Rosemary-Lavender and Sage

Hosta PRO ONLY

Lilac

Mega Pack #1 - Petals

Mega Pack #2 - Leaves

Orchid

Peony

Poinsettia

Poppy

Poppy PRO

Primrose

Roses

Roses PRO

Spider Plant PRO ONLY stencil

Star Lily

Sunflower

Sweet Pea

Tomato PRO ONLY

Tree Leaves

Tulip

Twig, blossom and leaves

Violets

Wild Rose

Xmas Leaf Selection

We bring out new stencils every month. The PRO stencils are long life based on a plastic material that can resist polymer clay. Standard stencils are normally card and need to be treated with baby oil and cleaned well after use to get multiple uses from them.

For details see our website

www.angiescarr.co.uk

Some self published books by other artists

Angie Scarr is a member of a Facebook group entitled

Self Publishing and Author Group (arts and crafts tutorials)

www.facebook.com/groups/selfpubauthors

Please support self published authors

Patreon

If you've never heard of Patreon before, imagine you could be a 'patron of the arts' in some small way helping your favourite artists to continue working inventing and teaching in their specialist area. Artists no matter how well known in their field often have no regular guaranteed income and often give away their inspiration for free because until now there wasn't an easy method to gain an income from day to day teaching, support and skill sharing.

This subscription service is an easy way to connect artist teachers with their students and followers, and as a way for the 'Patrons' to give the level of support they are comfortable with and receive in return (sometimes personalised) perks such as early access to new ideas, live patron only videos and little samples of work to help you visualise stages of work and qualities of colour. As well as advance knowledge of really new ideas before they ever get to publication. Some ideas of how I made things which never even reach the books which I call my 'daft ideas' for example how I made the awning for the Dollhouse shop on the front just using parts from an old umbrella! For benefit patrons I'm also able to send out little found 'things' which might inspire you, or samples of my new tools before they go into full production.

Many thanks to my current 50 plus patrons some of who have been with me for over a year now. You've all given me courage to start with new things like this book which has been put together in the year since I had your support and has been shared with you along the way. The Patreon thing has really helped me because its like having 50 sets of shoulders to lean on. 50 therapists and 50 special friends to share my daft ideas with and see if they work. Or at least are interesting enough for you not to walk away! 50 people who understand that no matter how well known an artist is they still may struggle from time to time. That's worth so much!

Thanks to: Anke Humpert, Gillian Mason Thompson, Linda Downs, Kasia Win, Robyn Stewart, Netta Murphy, Gill Bayes, Karin Sorensen, Denise Osborne, Karen Rollinson, Riemkje Boom, Jeanette Fishwick, Macie Kaye, Maryse Cuypers, Lesley Symons, Rachel Taylor, Tara Jane Susie Langworthy, Barbara Taylor Harris, Ann Storey, Natalie Martin Burrows, Helen Cruickshank, Stephanie Ryan, Cheryl la Greca Markov, Hellie Durans, Anne Erlandson Foss, Roberta Solari, Sandi Kluge-Smith, Robyn Stewart, Tee Bylo, Essie Kenneway *and others who do not wish to be mentioned.*

15% off retail orders on my site for patrons

Starting at only $1 per month, Patreon is my new subscription platform to allow my students and friends to support me and in return get a series of projects, little gifts and virtual and video peeks into my workshop on a day to day basis so that you get to know all the new ideas before anyone else does. Often before they're even fully formed! Your support will help me release more content and always to you first! This is such a young idea and such a new journey why not hop on with me and help me make it a success.

As an added bonus you'll be entitled to 15% off all purchases on my website, just mention Patreon in the additional details section of the order. If you are about to order anyway what have you got to lose?

www.patreon.com/angie_scarr

Suppliers

Flower wire

US Mary Kinloch sells flower wires and paper flower parts
www.ebay.com/str/tropicalminiaturesbymarykinloch

Also Michaels arts supplies in the US.
www.michaels.com

UK Vanilla valley
www.thevanillavalley.co.uk

Australia Ryans Realm
www.ryansrealm.com.au

or Lincraft (limited sizes available)
www.lincraft.com.au

Flower wire is always available from cake decorating suppliers

Houses and kits

For Dolls House shops in the UK
www.dollshousedirect.co.uk/dolls_houses

Shop kits USA Victoria Miniland
(Designed in the USA Manufactured in China)
www.miniland.ca

For more expensive tastes see a beautiful glass orangery
here.
www.nostalgische-puppenstuben.de/html/orangerien.html

Clay

Australia Over the Rainbow
polymerclay.com.au

USA Clay Factory Inc
www.clayfactoryinc.com

UK Clayaround
www.clayaround.com

Terracotta pots

from our website for small quantities
or Mibako for wholesale
mibako.galeon.com

Single sided blades

from us in sample packs or anywhere on ebay for large
packs

Vegetarian pill capsules

from us in sample packs or larger quantities via online
pharmacies or Amazon

Amazon affiliate scheme

We are a member and have links to many tools and materials, if you go through our website for all your Amazon
purchases we are paid a small commission which does not
affect your price

Biography

Angie Scarr started playing with polymer clay in the mid 1980s when she was in her 20s but it was in 1989 after her daughter was born and she quit a job as a social work assistant that she took up making miniatures more seriously, initially making the miniature foods for which she is better known. Angie's published ideas, though innovative at the time, are now part of the way miniatures are routinely made. Her work is now often copied, and as Angie herself readily admits, regularly equalled and often improved upon because she is not a perfectionist but the 'miniaturist's miniaturist' inventing methods for other artists to play with. Now in her 60s Angie doesn't want to stop coming up with what she (a Yorkshire woman now living in Andalusia in Spain) calls 'daft ideas' and carries on innovating solving three dimensional problems, finding short cuts and sharing inspirations and continues to have an influence on a new generation of miniature artists. This book is the culmination of another year of exploration into what polymer clay can do for the miniaturist.

For more biographical details and some of Angie & Frank's crazy adventures see her autobiographical book Making It Small available on Amazon as a paperback or ebook

Thanks and acknowledgements

Apart from the obvious help and inspiration and sometimes uncomfortable but kindly and invaluable criticism by my husband Frank. Thanks also go to: my daughter Kira for loads of support on Social Media Advertising etc. Absolutely vital these days. Who'd have thought little Kira would have grown up to be my Social Media Guru! To my brother Howie who makes me laugh makes me think and who it seems a has started to buy every one of my books which I know he would never have cause to read and by that action alone shows he cares!

To Mary Kinloch for allowing me to mooch around her Facebook group Making Dollshouse Flowers In All Scales, and for producing wonderful YouTube tutorials which inspired me. To other miniaturists who have in one way or another graciously said I've in some way inspired them including, but not exclusively the lovely and talented Gosia Suchudolska, the amazing Caroline McFarlane Watts of Tall Tales Productions.

The lovely Italians, Roberta Solari and Loredana Tonetti. My Danish Miniature Family - Birthe, Tina and Jonny of the Miniseum in Mariager. Cilla Hallbert who is like a Swedish sister to me. Agneta and Frederik from Skala Minimal in Sweden. Suzanne from Den Bosch fair in Holland and Tom Bishop for extra support when I needed it. Andrea Currie for constant help and her wonderful shop kit which I chopped and changed to my own whims and her husbands patience when I'd lost the information sheet and needed it pronto! There are many so many more friends who deserve a mention for their support. Many of them however appear on my Patreon page on p49 (those who are not too shy!) And many I know I've forgotten. Please forgive me! To all of you thanks for your love and support and if you're reading this thanks for helping keep me going by buying my book!

www.angiescarr.co.uk

For moulds, stencils, kits, books and other craft materials

www.facebook.com/angiescarr.miniatures
My facebook page where I let everyone know what is going on

www.instagram.com/angiescarr

www.youtube.com/user/angiescarr
for tutorials, howtos and videos about crafts and miniatures

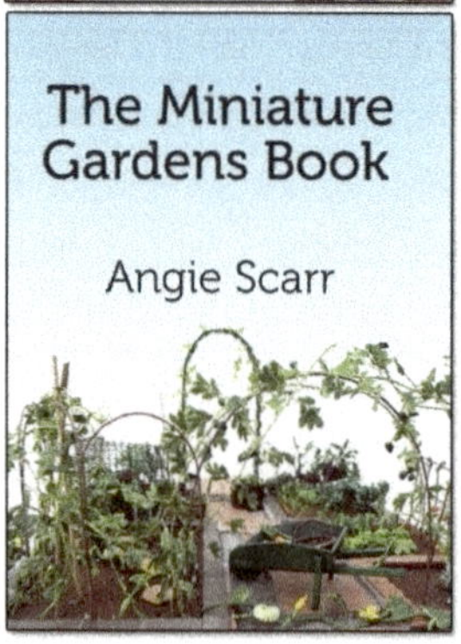

9 781687 037923